PENGUIN BOOKS

THE POWER OF MAKE-BELIEVE

Shouger Merchant Doshi, former journalist and juris doctor of law, Illinois, USA, always felt that she was lucky when it came to performing at job interviews or scoring a client. She later realized that this could only be attributed to her early childhood where she spent much time reading, writing and engaging in pretend play with her family members, which helped develop her communication skills. When she returned to Mumbai from the US, she noticed the same trajectory in other adults, of childhood playing patterns leading to enhanced communication skills. Yearning to bring awareness to this correlation, Shouger decided to leave the corporate world and found her passion in the children's space. It was also during the same time that she became a mother to her son, Kiaan. She co-founded two companies; the first, The Story Merchants, which manufactures children's educational products based on pretend play, and the second, The Pinwheel Project, an events company making children's products and services accessible pan-India. Armed with her literary prowess and breadth of knowledge on parenting, Shouger explores parenting through pretend play as an effective way to communicate, bond with and espouse intellectual development in the early years of your child's life.

ADVANCE PRAISE FOR THE BOOK

'*The Power of Make-Believe* is a book that every parent must have, particularly after persevering through the Covid-19 crisis. When we were in lockdowns with our children with little to no resources, we have all realized the power of make-believe and creativity while facing the difficulties of entertaining little ones in the confines of the house. The activities listed in the book require meagre resources, are fun, educational, have a great conversational element and there is a take-away from each one. The idea of using books and play to explain everyday phenomena is one that I very much endorse and practise even with my child. The recommended list of books is also very extensive and covers every topic. I highly recommend this book to parents who have children between 1–7 years of age for sure!'—**Soha Ali Khan, actor and author.**

'I have always believed in the power of real discourse with my kids over the standard parenting rat race stuff. The *Power of Make-Believe* hits home with my personal parenting principles. First, what parents do during their time with their young children has a major effect on their output later in life. Second, the best skill you can impart to your kids is the ability to reason and to have a great conversation on various topics with confidence.

'Creating your own path as a parent and having meaningful discussions with your child is an important centrepiece of forging their personality and raising a free and liberal thinker. Shouger Merchant Doshi crafts this book with equal doses of intellect and humour, and brings out a fresh perspective on parenting through pretend play. She shows how we can best impact our children's futures, their careers and choices in simple yet effective ways'—**Mini Mathur, actor and TV host.**

'As a mom, this book really resonated with me and was very special. It simply yet eloquently describes pretend play activities that mandates every parent to have various discussions with their child. Shouger has incorporated reading and good vocabulary practices in play, which truly helps in building the child's confidence. Children will be getting educated while playing and won't even realize it!

'*The Power of Make-Believe* is sure to be a winner for 2021, especially given the Covid-19 crisis that we are all going through. The book is a great way to immerse yourself in your children's world, while building good memories and skills that will benefit them as they grow'—**Amrita Raichand, chef.**

'One of the best parenting books out there; it doesn't preach or tell you what to do, instead tells you how you, as a parent, are that special someone who can impact your child's life by doing small but effective things at home to better engage, bond with and educate your child. Sure-shot winner'—Deepshikha Deshmukh, film producer.

'This book is an absolute delight; what I think hits the chord is the realization while reading that simple activities have such an impact on our children's growth and imagination. As a mom of three, I can vouch for the fact that becoming a mother is one of the best as well as the most challenging things that can happen to a woman. Moreover, since the lockdown due to Covid-19 continues to test parenting skills, this book will help immensely in keeping children purposefully busy while at home. The book will also help enhance your child's vocabulary with its many carefully curated activities, tips and tricks, and will enable many dinner table conversations with your children. In fact, this book is a result of the dinner table conversations Shouger had with her father; so one cannot emphasize enough the importance of meaningful conversations with your children. I highly recommend this book. It will be special for every child and parent'—Vinti Lodha, adviser, Lodha Luxury.

THE POWER OF MAKE-BELIEVE

PARENTING THROUGH PRETEND PLAY

SHOUGER MERCHANT DOSHI

PENGUIN BOOKS

An imprint of Penguin Random House

PENGUIN BOOKS

USA | Canada | UK | Ireland | Australia
New Zealand | India | South Africa | China | Singapore

Penguin Books is part of the Penguin Random House group of companies
whose addresses can be found at global.penguinrandomhouse.com

Published by Penguin Random House India Pvt. Ltd
4th Floor, Capital Tower 1, MG Road,
Gurugram 122 002, Haryana, India

Penguin
Random House
India

First published in Penguin Books by Penguin Random House India 2021

ISBN 9780143451891

Book design by Akangksha Sarmah
Chapter head illustrations by Rahael Mathews
Typeset in Adobe Caslon Pro by Manipal Technologies Limited, Manipal

Printed at Repro India Limited

www.penguin.co.in

MIX
Paper from
responsible sources
FSC® C047271

Growing up in a nuclear family, dinner table conversations were the most important time of the day. My sister and I always loved hearing stories of our father's childhood, the highs and lows of his past, and how he went from living in a room with fourteen family members to running a company with over 500 employees. He talked to us in adages, quotes and songs and told us plenty of old folktales and stories to inspire us to work hard and never take anything for granted. He was always giving us little nuggets of wisdom and found new stories each evening to delight us with. As we grew older, conversations turned to books—which we all were big fans of—artists, movements, theatre, music, politics, the state of the world and entrepreneurship. Our dining table was the one dining table in the world where the food placed on it was unimportant. We dissected several countries, spoke about the world wars, manufactured conflicts and created their resolutions, engaged in heated arguments and when not doing that, we would indulge in a great deal of jokes, laughter and love. Every point of view was heard and validated and never trivialized. There was a lot of value placed on knowledge, communication and critical thinking, which inspired us to form our own informed opinions on every aspect of life. Dad often quoted Steve Jobs, 'Don't let the noise of others' opinions drown out your inner voice.' So, to no one's surprise, we turned out to be big communicators!

While my father did not live long enough to have in-depth conversations with my son, I took it very seriously to continue his legacy and create an environment where the same open dialogue could be had with my child.

To my father, Arif A. Merchant—the world was a better place when you were at the head of the table. Thanks to those dinner table conversations with you, I found my voice as a writer and my pulse as a parent. Thank you for being the guiding light of my life.

#CONTENTS

PROLOGUE

It is a happy talent to know how to play.
—RALPH EMERSON

We, as modern parents, are a curious species indeed. Some of us spoil our children rotten, mainly to satisfy ourselves. Some of us wish to live out our unfulfilled aspirations and dreams through our children, desperately trying to teach them that one skill that we always wanted to pursue as children or young adults. To that end, we have pre-decided that our children will be toppers in their classes and will go on to become doctors or lawyers, without checking in on the inclination of the child. Some of us raise our children with the delusion that they must always be happy, so at the slightest crease of sadness on their faces, we offer them everything they want in the world to placate them. Another section of us feels that as long as our child is not crying, everything is going well, without ever bothering to have a conversation about feelings and emotions.

As parents, we have so many pre-determined aspirations for our children. When I had my son, everyone kept asking me many questions. What do you want him to be? Which school do you want him to go to? Which nursery is important for you to get into? Will you send him abroad to study? Are you gunning for Harvard? Would you want him to be a businessman, a professional or a 'creative type'? What kind of school programme are you looking for? Montessori? Playway? Waldorf?

I never had an answer to any of these questions. I had not thought that far ahead, and I figured my son would some day drive the conversation about what he wanted to do, what he enjoyed and that I would eventually figure out what he had a good skill set for. As far as the many kinds of school programmes go, I had only used the term Waldorf in relation to my salad and the fancy hotel in New York City.

But I always had an answer for one question: What kind of skill set do you want him to have?

I want him to be a confident child who can proficiently articulate his thoughts in a lucid, cogent and eloquent manner. That was all that was ever important to me. Having a good vocabulary and being able to use the power of the English language.

People scoffed.

They said you need to practise worksheets at home, reinforce the alphabet, take a phonics class, teach maths, enroll for certain singing classes that everyone was signing up for, teach him how to make a perfect circle, colour inside the lines, learn sequencing and solve puzzles every day. Only then would he perform well in the school interviews and be confident and have a good vocabulary.

I did not buy into the rat race, which made me feel guilty at times. I did not force him to attend all those classes or work on his alphabet, numbers and shapes. Instead, I spent hours with my son doing fun activities and dwelling in make-believe worlds. I spent time teaching him to play by himself while I worked, so he could explore learning in his own way because in my mind, *play* is the most essential form of *learning*. And who does not want to get lost in another world and explore new places? I know I did.

Now, a few years later, I am only too frequently told that my son is eloquent, well-spoken, expressive and can carry a good conversation. I am told he has a great memory and a good sense of the world and its belongings and people. His maths may not be that great and his ability to write has not fully developed yet, but I am not worried; I do not know a single adult who does not know how to write or do basic addition and subtraction. But I do know of adults who cannot confidently carry out a conversation.

I am often asked which classes did I enroll him in or whom did I go to for him to get here?

Mortified, I respond, 'We play.'

'What else?'

'We converse.'

'And?'

'We read.'

'Anything else?'

'We eat meals together and do household chores.'

They don't believe me.

One day, I was being interviewed on a news blog about how I keep my child busy at home while I attempt to work during the Covid-19 pandemic, and I revealed several pretend play activities that my son and I engage in on a weekly basis that help his visual processing skills and verbal comprehension. I was inundated with requests from people seeking more information on how they could do the same with their children and to share other role-play activities. And with the realization that not every parent knows how to *play with purpose*, the idea for this book was born.

Through this book, my goal is to share these pretend play activities with everyone so they can do these at home with their children. It is not rocket science though and you can easily come up with ones of your own if you have a creative predisposition, but these are tried-and-tested activities that have worked for me as a parent and have made parenting easier for me. These are not art and craft activities. At the same time, there are no activities without purpose. While there are several elements that involve art and craft, the concept is to give your child a better understanding of people and places in the world, and to engage them in a conversation—simply put: *playing with purpose*. It has various advantages and contributes to the overall development of a child. It is the best way for children and parents to bond, spark a conversation and learn through pretend play. All too often, you hear about or see parents buying expensive gadgets to encourage role-play—those mammoth kitchen sets, tents, doll houses and the works. I am guilty of that as well. But I assure you, it is a lot more fun to involve your child in the making and setting up of the activity. All the activities in this book contain minimal investment on your part and involve play with learning. You *can* teach numbers, alphabets, phonics, shapes, days, months, time, the weather cycle and the rest of the gamut—all through play and in a fun and exciting way!

A few things to keep in mind about this book:

* There are no pictures of the activities because I want you to know that your child's version of the activity is the best version of the activity. The artistic and visual appeal of the activity is only as good as the way your child makes it. The most important thing to keep in mind is the bond you

will create during the process of preparing for the activity. Think of it like the goal is to have fun while making the messiest, worst-tasting cake! But when you have the icing strewn all over you and your little one's face, and you share a laugh—those are the moments that make memories. So, there is no need to google away and find an image that corresponds with the activity; just follow the basic steps and feel free to tweak them to suit the needs of your child.

- I am surrounded by boys in my life—my husband, my son, my dog (also male)—and I do love being the lady of the house. Although being a parent to my calm and loyal bichon frise and to my hyperactive superhero-obsessed son are two very different things, except that both their appetites seem to be voracious. In this book, I will be using the male pronouns to refer to your child. Though I firmly believe in the equality of sexes and I do believe that I am an empowered woman, this usage is merely because I relate my son to every child.
- The activities are listed as if they are meant for one child because if you, like me, chose to be 'one and done', then these are all activities your child can do with your supervision and your guidance alone. If you have more than one child, the more the merrier. While the activities require a little bit of planning and organization at your end, the end result is well worth the effort and will be palpably apparent to you over time. My plea is that you look at these activities as an opportunity to bond with your child while they are home (or forced to be at home) and as an educational yet exciting way to converse about worldly phenomena and happenings and watch them absorb, process and rationalize.

✳ The one thing that is crucial to note in this book and in life is that there are no rules in the circus that is parenting and there is no sure-shot guide that will make you a better parent. Parenting is a complex process where listening to your child, figuring things out by a process of trial and error, and putting in place the processes that work for you is the best approach. We are all in this together, winging it and taking it one day at a time. So, while I have outlined some parenting parameters that I have researched and that have helped me become a happier, balanced and more confident parent, the things that I swear by, they are not universal guidelines to parenting. But I hope this book will help make those moments with the small human in your life count and full of purposeful fun.

CHAPTER 1

#WhyPretendPlay

The debt we owe to the play of imagination is incalculable.
—KARL JUNG

$$\approx$$

Play comes in many different forms. Researchers have segregated them into skill-based play forms such as fine motor or gross motor skill play or based them on the nature of the play, such as cooperative play, while others have classified them according to the number of people playing together. However, all forms of play, when coupled with a vivid imagination, storytelling or narration, constitute pretend play, which is an unparalleled form of early learning for children.

Some researchers call it dramatic play, role-play, exploratory play, fantasy play, symbolic play, creative play—I simply call it 'pretend play'. It is multi-dimensional and incorporates all the elements of structured and unstructured play.

Children need to develop a variety of skill sets to optimize the process of their growth. Research and experts have always indicated that dramatic play with family members and peers is significant in igniting social, emotional, cognitive, language and visual processing skills that create decision-making and overall brain development. So, when your child wants to play Doctor-Doctor and operate on you, don't consider it a waste of time. You will be surprised with what he is learning from that.

Children learn by imagining and doing. They learn by talking about concepts in their own words—when they are allowed to express themselves in the way that they have learnt, by observing people around them. In fact, it is not just about a sense of self-expression, but a deeper and more logical processing of sorts that occurs when children take on pretend play.

So why is pretend play the foremost and most effective way to inculcate key early learning skills in children? The number of ways in which children develop and grow while engaged in rich creative play is countless and incorporates every early learning skill imaginable. Here are some to help you understand its value in well-rounded child development:

1. Despite the name, pretend play is *not frivolous*. As per the American Academy of Pediatrics, it is proven to boost brain structure and function and promote self-regulatory functions, which allow children to focus on their goals and ignore distractions.

2. It helps children develop their *imagination skills*. They learn to be *creative* and think out of the box using the tools at hand, creating what they require and building fantastical items and stories using what they have.

3. It helps children expand their *vocabulary*. They engage in realistic *language development*—talking to each other, listening, asking questions, incorporating words and

phrases they have heard—and practise having a 'real' adult conversation.

4. When pretend play involves more than one child, it can also encourage children to mimic and practise the important art of *conferring with each other*, *sharing* and *taking turns*, all of which teach them collaboration and healthy competition—important life lessons to learn.

5. When they are engaged in pretend play, children build important burgeoning skills and get practical experience in *sorting*, *classifying* and *organizing* items according to size, colour, utility, variety, etc. and in creating something larger with them.

6. Pretend play helps children *self-regulate* and leads to better decision-making and problem-solving.

7. Pretend play helps expand a child's *attention span* while they are planning the play; their attention tends to last longer during pretend play than any other kind of play since they have put an effort into creating it.

8. It fosters *leadership qualities*. Ever notice your child say, 'I will get it and do it, close your eyes'? That is your child saying he wants to be a leader. Discussing the pretend play activities will help your child become more independent and eventually he will want to take charge, control and direct the activities, thereby fostering essential leadership qualities.

9. Enacting something has a huge impact on your child's *language* and *literacy skills*. Have you ever heard your child engage in imaginary play with his toys or friends? You will possibly hear some words and phrases that you would have never thought he knew! In fact, you will often hear your own words reflected in your children's pretend play. Your child can

perhaps do a perfect simulation of all the people he is around on a day-to-day basis! If he is given a chance to process what he has been absorbing around him, through pretend play, it will help him understand the power of language. Furthermore, pretend play gives your child a command over the spoken word, helps him articulate and express himself, and enables him to piece together what he has heard in a constructive way. This process helps your child to not only increase his vocabulary and language skills, but also to make a connection between the spoken and the written word.

10. Pretend play evinces an aspect of *social and emotional skills*. When your child engages in pretend play, he is actively investigating the social and emotional roles in life. Through cooperative play, he learns how to take turns, share responsibility and creatively problem-solve. When your child pretends to be different characters, it teaches him empathy and decision-making. It is normal for young children to see the world through their own point of view, but through their developmental process and play, your child will begin to understand others' feelings.

11. Pretend play fosters *problem-solving* and *independence*. Pretend play provides your child with a variety of problems to solve. Whether it's two children wanting to play the same role or searching for the right material to make tent walls, your child utilizes important cognitive skills. It also builds self-esteem when your child finds that he can be anything just by pretending!

12. It helps develop essential *life skills* such as adjusting, being cooperative, *and* the ability to deal with various situations and tackle them in different ways.

Pretend play as an early learning tool makes way for increased cognitive abilities in older children. Notable studies conducted by lauded researchers with controlled focus groups have shown the following conclusions:

1. Major cognitive growth takes place from the age of two through seven, which stems from perceptions created during pretend play.

2. Pretend play allows the expression of positive and negative feelings, which later gives way to emotional intelligence.

3. Make-believe games are precursors to the important capacity for self-regulation, including reduced aggression, delay of gratification, concern and empathy.

4. An important benefit of early pretend play is the child's enhanced capacity for cognitive flexibility, adaptability and aptitude in later stages of his life.

5. Early imaginative play had a positive relation to increased creative performance in later years. For example, Robert Root-Bernstein's research with exceptionally creative individuals such as Nobel Prize winners and the MacArthur Foundation's Genius Grant awardees, indicates that games about make-believe worlds were more frequent in early childhood of such individuals than other ordinary participants, thus making it clear that pretend play indeed lends a creative predisposition.

All in all, one can only glean advantages from pretend play and no disadvantages whatsoever, so give it a go! As parents, this will give you the satisfaction of knowing that you are investing in your child's future betterment. More than anything, it is also an excellent way to bond with your child and relive moments of your own childhood!

CHAPTER 2

#Let'sPrepToPlay

Children learn as they play. Most importantly,
in play children learn to learn.
—O. FRED DONALDSON

To make pretend play effective, there are a few things that are supremely important. Planning and preparation for the activities must be viewed positively. There are a few guidelines to keep in mind:

1. *Selection*: To begin, select either an activity and a concept that the child is interested in or a setting that they are familiar with, so their engagement with the activity is natural and enjoyable. For example, if your child is particularly interested in dump trucks and diggers, you can select a construction site as an activity. Sometimes, you can also be led by what he is learning in school. If he has mentioned community helpers or modes of transport as a topic being discussed in school, then go with that.

2. *Make Time:* As a working mother, I get limited hours in the day with my son; so it is important to make these hours count. Spending time together, discussing certain life lessons, telling him about your day, fixing a snack together, doing some yoga, playing a board game, etc. are all ways of bonding with your child. Pretend play, however, incorporates many different skills—fine motor skills, gross motor skills, vocabulary, social and cognitive skills, memory, mathematics and much more. So, when you plan these activities, it is not all fun, it's play with a purpose.

3. *Create Stories:* Stories are most important in pretend play. Tell your child different stories. You could, for example, read about construction workers a night before, get your child excited about the topic and involve them in making a pretend construction site and in acting like a construction worker. Once they have heard the story from you, their minds will start churning and they will start conceptualizing.

4. *Research:* If your child is interested in science and wants to know more about the solar system for example, take him to the planetarium, read up on the topic and then undertake the pretend play activity on the solar system.

5. *Encourage Further Exploration:* If your child wants to take the activity towards a different direction, encourage it and allow him to take off on a new tangent to encourage his confidence and improve his self-esteem. You could then slowly bring him back to the task at hand and draw his attention to the activity.

6. *Materials*: Ask your child to help by fetching the materials and figuring out their use. For example, you may have marbles at your home that may be used for decorative purposes, but when you pretend play, you could use them as pebbles, or you may have crepe paper at home that you perhaps got as part of a gift—ask your child questions like: 'Do you think it would be a good idea to shred it and use it as a base for this basket?' Asking them to think out of the box, fetch the materials themselves, organize them and creatively classify them, helps engender their creative skills.

7. *Create Writing Opportunities:* Within the pretend play, there may be opportunities where some writing can be encouraged. For example, when signs need to be made for the pretend coffee shop or perhaps a list for grocery shopping, ask them to help you spell the words or make them write it, if they are able to. When they do write, praise them so they are encouraged to write and explore the written word more.

8. *Question Them*: As they play, ask them open-ended questions and encourage them to make-believe. You could ask questions such as: What do you do with this? How does that work? What do you do next? What are you planning to do during the day? Which activity are you doing? What happens after that? Which items do you require? Make use of both verbs and nouns, and try to use descriptive words when you speak about things and explain their meanings. Their brains are like sponges and somewhere in there, everything you say is being processed and registered.

9. *Correct Them When They Make Mistakes:* If you are doing a pretend construction-worker play and your child says he is

making the plans for the building, you should inform him that it is an architect's job to make the design plans for the building, while the engineer does the technical work to make sure the architect's design works and the construction worker is the one who actually builds the building. So, this way, he learns beyond the periphery of the specific concept.

10. *Incorporate Learning and School Work into the Role-Play:* You can practise *numbers* by asking them to count the number of tools or fetch a specific number of items for the pretend play. You can incorporate *shapes* while drawing or creating patterns with the items you have. You can incorporate fine motor skills and gross motor skills by asking your child to hold, press, sift or put together things, depending on what the activity is.

11. *Let Them Lead You:* Once you explain the concept to the child, they may want to lead the process and do things differently. The activity is for them to learn to take charge and make use of their personal experience to do certain things. Let them enjoy the setting-up process as well as the play process in their own way, with light suggestions from you.

12. *Do Not Denigrate Them*: The beauty of their creation or the aptness of their enactment is not important. It is the method of expression, the planning and the preparation. You may nudge them here and there, but do not do things for them; do not lead them and if they err, definitely do not criticize their creation or the direction that they manifested. Instead, provide them with the background information necessary for them to take things forward and show you their expression of the concept.

Here is a list of resources that you will need to pretend play at home effectively:

a. Cardboard sheets or pieces
b. Cardboard boxes (discarded boxes from Amazon, Flipkart, etc. will work)
c. Chart paper or regular paper
d. Tape
e. Glue
f. Crayons, colour pencils, water colours

Here is a list of things you should endeavour to save and stock your craft cupboard with, so your child can more creatively engage in the pretend play activities:

a. Confetti
b. Pompoms
c. Ice-cream sticks
d. Lids of any kind
e. Fabric pieces
f. Paper plates
g. Cups
h. Rubber bands
i. Coloured paper strips
j. Toothpicks
k. Wrapping paper
l. Shoelaces or ribbons
m. Cotton
n. Shells
o. Beads (beads from discarded artificial jewellery can work)

p. Bubble wrap

q. Rocks, pebbles or marbles

r. Glitter packets or sticks

s. Stickers

t. Toilet paper rolls

u. Paper clips

v. Bedsheets

w. Empty spray bottles

In the next few chapters, you can explore **more than sixty pretend play activities** that are extremely fun and engaging; they contain educational content, are easy to put together and have a rich learning curve. Enjoy!

CHAPTER 3

#ActivitiesForTheWin

The playing adult steps sideward into another reality; the playing child advances forward to new stages of mastery.
—ERIK H. ERIKSON

This chapter explores activities that involve fine and gross motor skills in addition to cognitive and language development, and are ideal for the age group of three to seven years.

1. MINIATURE SCHOOL

Going to school can be a daunting experience, primarily because children don't know what to expect in school. Creating a miniature pretend school and going through the motions of what happens in a school can create less apprehension and help them associate school with a more positive atmosphere.

#WhatYouNeed

- ☞ A shoebox
- ☞ Tape
- ☞ Colour pencils, water colours
- ☞ Chart paper, scissors, glue
- ☞ Miniature figurines (Peppa Pig, superheroes, Legos, etc.)
- ☞ Any transparent plastic sheet

#HowtoPrep

✻ Cut open the lid of the shoebox and stick a transparent plastic sheet on top of the box so you can see the inside.

✻ On one side of the box, ask your child to write the name of his pretend school, and his class and division to create writing and identification opportunities.

✻ Cut out the base of the shoebox to make square windows. You can then outline them with coloured washi tape or mounting tape, or draw designs along their borders. You can also cut out a rectangular door from the base of the shoebox and then tape it on one side so it opens and closes.

✻ Inside the box is your classroom. Ask your child what the layout of his classroom is. If it has a whiteboard or a blackboard, then you can stick one inside using chart paper. You may ask him to write or draw something on the board as well. Ask him if there are posters of the planets, animals, children, etc. on the walls of his classroom, and then encourage him to try drawing those posters. You can stick them on the sides of the shoebox.

* Finally, if you have miniature doll's house furniture such as chairs and tables, use them to furnish the classroom. You can alternatively make the chairs, benches and tables using thermocol, clay or cardboard. You may also place miniature figurines as students and teachers in the classroom.

#HowtoPlay

* Let your child lead this one since he is the one in school. Let him act out situations in his classroom and play with the characters he has placed there; he may assume the role of the teacher and talk to the children; he may base the characters on his friends in school or outside it. Let him move them in and out of the classroom, have someone spill their lunch over their clothes, or go to the bathroom, look out the window, forget their homework at home, etc.

* Use this shoe box as a 'busy box' whenever your child wants to play by himself and keep himself busy. Also, if you listen to him playing, you will find out a lot more about what goes on in your child's school or what his fears about going to one are.

#KeySkills

☞ Creative thinking and imagination skills
☞ Role-play expression
☞ Vocabulary enhancement
☞ Visual comprehension skills

2. MINI CONSTRUCTION SITE

Getting to know our surroundings is an important part of understanding them. We often see construction sites filled with construction vehicles and men wearing yellow hard hats; these sites are often accompanied by loud noises that could scare a child. Taking your child to a real construction site before beginning this activity or reading a book about the different materials and machines that are used in a construction site such as cement, concrete, bricks, cranes, bulldozers, etc., would be a great start.

#WhatYouNeed

- Sand (kinetic sand will do as well)
- Pebbles or stones or marbles or beads
- Miniature construction vehicles and figurines
- A black marker
- A large cardboard box or tray
- Chart paper
- Toothpicks
- Paper, glue and scissors
- Colour pencils
- Cotton (optional)

#HowtoPrep

- In the cardboard box or tray, pour the sand unevenly and spread the pebbles or stones over it.
- Place the miniature construction vehicles on different sides of the box.

✳ Next, colour two white sheets in blue (or use blue chart paper) for the back of the box and draw buildings on it with a black marker. Use some cotton for clouds and you can also draw or stick a cut-out of the sun.

✳ Draw and colour two 'STOP' signs. Cut them out and stick them on two toothpicks. Place them on different sides in the middle of the box.

✳ You can also make up other signs. Use chart paper to make tent cards (triangular shaped and self-standing) and place them on the floor of the box. The tent cards could say things such as 'CONSTRUCTION WORK AHEAD' or 'GO SLOW'.

✳ If you have mini construction cones or other toy road signs at home, you can place them in the pretend site as well. You now have your construction site ready.

#HowtoPlay

✳ Ask your child to take out any miniature characters or figurines that he may have at home, then place them in the box and start weaving stories about the construction site. Through pretend play, it would be prudent to slip into the conversation about how a plot of land or construction permits are acquired, and make clear the roles of designers, architects, engineers and construction workers and the materials they use, so your child can use that information in the formation of his stories.

#KeySkills

- ᵇ Gross motor skills
- ᵇ Logical reasoning
- ᵇ Creative and imagination skills
- ᵇ Vocabulary and language development
- ᵇ Writing skills

3. SPACE SHUTTLE FUN

Children are fascinated by outer space and everything that comes with it. So, if your child has been asking a lot of questions about planets or asteroids or meteors, this activity is a good one for the books.

#WhatYouNeed

- ᵇ **Aluminium foil**
- ᵇ **Paper, chart paper**
- ᵇ **Pens, water colours, tape, glue**
- ᵇ **Cornflour**
- ᵇ **Sand**
- ᵇ **Stamps or stickers of stars**

#HowtoPlay

- ✳ Read up about space. Explain some of the concepts to your child so that they can try and envision what outer space looks like, the objects that are in it and how they function.

✳ To help him understand it better, tell your child he can make an outer-space mood board.

✳ Paint a large chart paper black or purple to form your solar system. Place it flat on your table or on the floor to dry.

✳ Cut out lots of stars in the shapes of constellations and paste them on the chart paper once it dries. You may select constellations such as the Big Dipper, Orion, etc. and model the star clusters according to their pattern. If you have stamps or stickers, you can use those as well.

✳ You can also paste Aluminium foil balls (in different sizes) to resemble moon rocks, asteroids or meteors.

✳ Do not forget the yellow sun, the white or silver moon and the nine planets! You may include Pluto, but explain to your child that it is not considered a planet anymore as science is constantly evolving and new evidence suggests that it is not a planet. While outlining, colouring and sticking the planets on chart paper, keep the children engaged by telling them about the various attributes of each planet. For instance, Mercury is the hottest one as it is closest to the sun; Venus is the brightest one; Saturn has many rings; Earth is where we live and so on.

✳ Once you have all this in place, you can paste some moon sand on the moon using kinetic sand or simply some mud mixed with water and cornflour.

✳ You may also paste a few spaceships on the mood board— draw, colour and cut them out of chart paper, like all the others.

✳ Your child can use this mood board to pretend teaching science, explain the various elements and as he gets more interested in the galaxy, he will develop creative stories around it.

#KeySkills

- ☞ Visual processing skills
- ☞ Sensory motor skills
- ☞ Visual comprehension skills
- ☞ Creative and imagination skills
- ☞ Cognitive reasoning skills

4. DO-IT-YOURSELF LAUNDROMAT

Which child is not fascinated by the rolling and rumbling of a washing machine? How do clothes go in dry and dirty and come out clean? Allow them to undertake this activity to find out more about laundry!

#WhatYouNeed

- ☞ **Two huge cartons**
- ☞ **Colour pens**
- ☞ **A clothes basket with a lot of clothes**
- ☞ **Some towels**
- ☞ **Paper; water colours or crayons**

☞ **Scissors**
☞ **Chart paper**

#HowtoPrep

✹ Cut out circular doorways from both the cartons and put a paper flap for a handle. One can be the washer and the other the dryer.

✹ You can paint, colour or draw the various signages on the top of the washing machine and the dryer.

✹ Keep a tray or a laundry bag full of pretend soap cubes. To make them, you can cut and fold a white chart paper to form a six-sided cube by gluing all the sides together. You can write 'Soap' on it and place ten to twelve of them in a tray on top of the washing machine.

✹ Place all the clothes your child wishes to wash in the laundry basket. Your child may take some of your clothes as well to "clean", but as long as they are having fun and learning, it should be all right.

#HowtoPlay

✹ Whenever your child changes his clothes, get him into the habit of putting them into the laundry basket. In case he wants to wash his clothes himself, you do not want them pressing all the wrong buttons on the real washing machine. So pretend play washer-dryer to the rescue!

✹ Tell him to separate the clothes in the laundry basket according to their colour and size, and wash each load in the pretend play washing machine with a paper cube of soap. Once they are washed, ask him to put them into the dryer without dropping them on the floor.

✳ You can also incorporate a numbers and colours' test while sorting the clothes.

✳ If your child is above five years of age, you can include a cash register, some coins and bills for change in their pretend play laundry. So, each time you want to get them to wash your clothes, you can pay them, have them write you a bill and come back to collect your clothes once they have been washed, dried and put in a hanger by your child. It is a good way to teach them numbers and denominations of currency, and to explain the procedure followed in a professional laundry service and the exchange of money and services.

#KeySkills

☞ Creative and imagination skills
☞ Logical reasoning skills
☞ Visual processing skills
☞ Independence, self-reliance and confidence-building skills
☞ Role-play expression

5. GINGERBREAD HOUSE

The quintessential Christmas Eve gift would be a gingerbread house. What if your child could make it himself and derive so much more meaning from it? After all, if he wants presents from Santa, he must work hard to please him.

#WhatYouNeed

- ⊳ Cardboard sheets
- ⊳ An old board game (optional)
- ⊳ Water colours
- ⊳ Paper, red chart paper, superglue
- ⊳ Colour pencils
- ⊳ Miniature figurines

#HowtoPlay

✻ In the week leading up to Christmas, cut out a large cardboard piece for the base of the gingerbread house, of approximately 20 x 25 inches. Then cut out two long rectangular pieces and two short ones for the sides.

✻ For the roof, you can either use an old board game, a piece of folded cardboard or even a simple red chart paper. Stick it on top using superglue.

✻ Remember to keep the roof open from one side so it can be lifted to look inside the house.

✻ Draw (or print) various candies, cakes, doughnuts, ice creams and sweets. You may also use candy wrappers. Now stick them on the roof.

✻ Ask your child to draw round windows on the sides of the house in the shape of lollipops. Also cut out a door in the cardboard house.

✻ Once the glue has dried and the house is standing on its own, your child can paint the entire house, draw flowers, snow, a gingerbread man, etc. on the house and use miniature characters in the house. He could make up interesting stories about the gingerbread man and his house.

- The important thing is to keep it under your Christmas tree on Christmas Eve and let Santa fill his gingerbread house with all things sweet (use the lift flap on the roof to fill it).

#KeySkills

- Creative and imagination skills
- Cognitive reasoning skills
- Motor skill development
- Role-play expression
- Vocabulary and language development

6. CITY MAPPING

If you, like Robert Frost, want to take the road less travelled, then you need to know the roads well enough! Teaching your child where they live, to be aware of their surroundings and how to get from one place to another is significant. This activity is an easy way to start getting them interested in their surroundings.

#WhatYouNeed

- A few sheets of paper
- Tape
- Crayons
- Miniature cars and figurines

#HowtoPrep

✳ Take a few sheets of paper and tape them together to create one long rectangular sheet.

✳ On this, draw a rough map of the city you live in—for example, draw two 3-inch roads running through the entire map, along which you can draw squares, labelling them clearly to indicate what they represent. Remember to leave the insides of these squares empty. The squares could represent the following places: a coffee shop, a movie theatre, a bookstore or toy store known to your child, his school, a playground, a sport complex, a bank, a grocery store, a doctor's clinic, a hospital, a vet's clinic, restaurants, ice-cream stores, etc.

✳ You can put in other places that may be of interest to your child such as a post office, a police station, a construction site, etc.

✳ Once you have made an outline of each place and labelled them adequately, ask your child to draw inside the squares. For a coffee shop, he may draw a mug or a table and a chair for people to sit on. For a school, he may draw a blackboard and tables and chairs. It does not really matter what he draws, as long as it is an interpretation of the location for him.

✳ Your child may draw a garden, paint the roads grey and white, add some traffic lights on the roads, draw the sea and colour it.

✳ Take your time making this map because it can be used for quite a while.

#HowtoPlay

✸ Once the map is ready, your child can put all his miniature figurines and vehicles at various places on the map. If he has an ambulance, ask him to place it inside the hospital. If you have a chef figurine, ask him to place it inside the restaurant and so on.

✸ Now, using this map as a pretend play board, start by telling your child a story that uses all the places, vehicles and characters on the board. Then, let him use your story as a catalyst and continue imagining more details and spins using the board.

✸ For example, my son drew a jail cell inside the police station on the board and all his stories were about the policeman catching the robbers who kept stealing from all the stores.

#KeySkills

☞ Creative and imagination skills
☞ Information processing skills
☞ Language development skills
☞ Problem-solving skills
☞ Independence, self-reliance and confidence-building skills

7. BABY NURSERY

Caring for a child is not an easy job. Teaching children how to care for others early in life makes them more compassionate and emotionally evolved. Once your child has outgrown his baby needs—bottles, diapers, feeding chairs, pacifiers, rattles and bibs—this activity is perfect for them to do.

#WhatYouNeed

- Milk bottles
- Diapers
- Tray or boxes
- Clipboard
- Bibs
- Rattles
- Books
- Two cardboard boxes or crates
- Markers, glue, tape
- Baby clothes
- Sheets of paper
- Baby dolls
- Towels
- A spray pump with water

#HowtoPrep

- Arrange all the items in neatly labelled trays or boxes.
- Take a clipboard and attach a 'check-in' sheet on which your child has to write the name and age of each child (baby doll) that comes into the baby nursery.
- Make a list on a sheet of paper with the following items: Diaper change, Reading, Bath time, Play time, Nap time,

Feeding time. When each activity is completed, the child can just check it off the list.

* Place a changing mat or a sheet for the changing station.
* Keep some toys (rattles, light-up toys, miniature cars, dolls, etc.) and books in a separate tray or box.
* Place a small tub and towel for Bath time, along with a spray pump filled with water. Keep the baby clothes at the ready too.
* Place some bedsheets inside a cardboard box or a crate to resemble a doll's bed.
* Ready some milk bottles for Feeding time.

#HowtoPlay

* Tell your child that he has to treat each doll like a real baby.
* He has to ensure he does all of it—first change the doll's diaper (you may need to teach him how to do this first), then the baby and your child can play with the toys, following which, the baby can be put to sleep in the bed. After a while, ask your child to check on the baby, who has now woken up, ask him to remove the baby's clothes and bathe him with a spray water bottle. Then dry the baby with a towel and put him in a new set of clothes.
* He also has to feed the baby with the milk bottle or else he will get hungry and start crying.
* Once all the different baby stations are full, your child can no longer accept any more babies into the nursery.

✳ When you come to pick up your baby, please thank your child for the caring and considerate way in which he has looked after your baby.

#KeySkills

☞ Social and emotional skills
☞ Logical thinking skills
☞ Rational thinking skills
☞ Role-play expression

8. NATURE TRAIL

Get your children to fall in love with nature and all its miracles by doing this simple activity!

#WhatYouNeed

☞ Brown paper
☞ Water colours, crayons, markers, scissors, glue, tape
☞ Paper and clipboard
☞ A notebook
☞ A pair of binoculars
☞ A magnifying glass and a measuring tape
☞ A water bottle, a cap, sunblock, a bag
☞ A glass jar

#HowtoPrep

✳ Showing him a documentary on nature is a good way to introduce him to the realm of nature. Once he is excited about exploring nature, he will want to undertake this pretend play nature trail with you.

✳ Prior to undertaking this trail, you may also read up on the outdoors—about campsites, trails and hikes, birds and animals that can be found on a trail and the various kinds of flowers, trees and plants that one can spot. While your child may not spot any of these on the pretend trail in a garden or around the neighbourhood, he will attempt to look for them, which will increase his cognitive and visual processing skills and sharpen his recall.

✳ First, draw a vest on brown paper and cut it out. Colour in some badges and stick them all over the vest. Wear a cap, some sunblock and dress like you are going for a hike to get into the mood even if you are only going for a walk around the block.

✳ Next, pack a bag. Take a bottle of water, a magnifying glass, an explorer's journal (notebook) and a pair of binoculars (can also be made by sticking two toilet paper cardboad rolls together and painting them). The explorer's journal is where your child can record findings.

✳ Now, get out of the house with your child and go for a walk. This is going to be your nature trail.

#HowtoPlay

* On the trail, your child should be tasked with check-marking his observations in his explorer's journal. The following list is based on a basic city hike; you can add more outdoor elements if you are out of the city.
    * Find and collect a purple flower.
    * Find and collect four pebbles or rocks.
    * Spot a dragonfly.
    * Spot an ant or an anthill.
    * Spot a bird.
    * Spot a butterfly.
    * Spot twelve leaves and collect them.
    * Spot a worm.
    * Spot a caterpillar.
    * Spot a dog.
    * Spot a bird's nest.
    * Spot five twigs and collect them.
    * Spot a squirrel.
    * Count the clouds.
    * Count the trees.
    * Collect a specimen of mud.
* Once they have checked all of the above, they can be brought back home and they have to use their collections from their nature trail. In their journal, they can write about each item they saw and collected in detail.

✳ They can also make use of the various items they have collected. Help them measure each item with a measuring tape and record it in the journal with the correct labelling. The pebbles and rocks can be washed and painted upon. The twigs can be used with play dough to make a character or something else. He can use the leaves to create a pattern in his journal, by painting and impressing the leaves onto the pages. The flowers can be pressed and pasted in the journal and your child may draw a scenery around them.

✳ The easiest thing to do would be to create a terrarium. Use any glass jar and put in the mud, the pebbles, the leaves and the flowers to make a miniature garden. Terrariums are meant to bring good luck. They can be placed outside the door or on a window ledge and will remind your child of this nature trail. This will make him look forward to spending more time with nature.

#KeySkills

- ☞ Sensory motor skills
- ☞ Visual comprehension skills
- ☞ Creative and imagination skills
- ☞ Self-reliance
- ☞ Logical thinking skills

9. RACE CAR TRACK

For all the car lovers, this is a great activity to use those toy cars to do something slightly more constructive with them!

#WhatYouNeed

- ☞ Felt or rubber mats
- ☞ Water colours and brushes
- ☞ Miniature vehicles and figurines
- ☞ Cardboard
- ☞ Ice-cream sticks
- ☞ Play dough

#HowtoPlay

* Cut a rubber or felt mat into some squares and rectangles. You will also need two U-shaped cut-outs. These represent the roads, which can be joined to form an oval racetrack for the cars. Paint the pieces black or grey. Then take some white paint and mark a few lane lines in the middle of each road.

* Next, take the ice-cream sticks and draw three circles on them in red, yellow and green to resemble traffic lights. Take the play dough and make funnel-shaped bases for the ice-cream sticks so that they can stand on their own. Place them at various intervals along the racetrack.

* You can also create bridges by bending cardboard pieces and painting them any colour you want. You may put the two ends of the bridge on similar funnel-shaped stands

we used for the traffic lights, to ensure the bridge stays in place. Place these bridges wherever you want.

✳ Next, place your cars around the track.

✳ The best part about this is that it is portable. Pack the entire thing into your child's busy bag and take it along on your travels.

✳ This is a great activity to engage in dramatic play with. You can make a zebra crossing and place miniature characters on it as well. Children can learn a great deal about traffic rules with these. You may also use U-turn and No Parking signs.

#KeySkills

↪ Motor skill development
↪ Logical reasoning skills
↪ Creative and imagination skills
↪ Visual processing skills

10. LAVA LAMP SCIENCE EXPERIMENT

There are many fun science experiments you can try with your child to get them curious about the world of science. Something as simple as adding baking soda to vinegar in a bottle can inflate a balloon and children cannot get enough of it. Try the lava lamp experiment; it is an exciting introduction to the world of science.

#WhatYouNeed

- ☞ A clean plastic bottle
- ☞ A cup of water, funnels, droppers, test tubes
- ☞ Vegetable oil and food colouring
- ☞ Alka Selzer or any fizzing tablet
- ☞ Lab coat

#HowtoPlay

✴ Get your child dressed as a scientist with a lab coat and some protective goggles. Arrange for a couple of beakers, measuring jars, funnels, droppers, test tubes, etc. for him to play and measure the water and the oil prior to the experiment.

✴ Fill a bottle with a little water.

✴ Pour the vegetable oil in the bottle until it is almost full. You can use a measuring cup with a spout or a funnel to make it more fun. As you watch, you will see the water and oil separating and the oil floating on the surface of the water.

✴ Add a few drops of your favourite food colouring. Watch as the colour sinks through the oil.

✴ Once the colouring has spread, break your fizzing tablet in half and drop it into the bottle. Watch your child be amazed as the bubbly globules form!

✴ Turn the bottle up and down to watch the bubbles form, and at night, turn off the lights and drop in the other half of the tablet. This time, shine the flashlight through the lava lamp while it is still bubbling! You can even keep it on top of your night light so your lava lamp shines through the night.

✸ Your child will enjoy looking at it daily with the satisfaction of having created an addition to his room.

#KeySkills

☞ Logical reasoning
☞ Cognitive development
☞ Visual processing skills
☞ Creative skills
☞ Problem-solving skills

11. CARDBOARD CUBBY

Everyone needs that one cozy space that they can go to for comfort. How about creating one such space for your child? This activity is a must in every household.

#WhatYouNeed

☞ A large cardboard box (you can make it in the shape of a rocket, a house or a castle, depending on the height and width of the box you get)
☞ Markers, pen, paper
☞ Blankets, cushions
☞ Books
☞ Fairy lights (optional)

#HowtoPlay

✳ Paint a carboard box in the colour your child likes. Cut out a large space for your child so he can fit inside comfortably. Layer the inside roof with fairy lights and the bottom with throws, blankets and cushions; add some books. Ensure the back of the box is sealed shut and it is only open from the front. You can also place a boombox for some music. You can ask your child to draw and paint or colour the insides of the box. You can write your child's name on the box, for example, REHAAN'S COZY CUBBY.

✳ Place it in a corner of your child's room and you have a snug little reading or relaxing corner for your child.

✳ Children love to take ownership of a space. So, this activity is great for when your child needs some quiet and alone time.

✳ If your child is at an age where he is fascinated with all things magical—paint or create a small 4-inch door in one corner of the Cozy Cubby and tell him that fairies come in through that door (especially the tooth fairy for when he loses a tooth).

#KeySkills

☞ Creative thinking and imagination skills
☞ Rational thinking skills
☞ Self-reliance and independence
☞ Writing and motor skills
☞ Social and emotional skills

12. CAR WASH TUNNEL

If you have taken your child into a car wash tunnel, you know it is supremely exciting for them. Telling them to create one at home and getting their creative juices flowing is a great way to spend a Sunday afternoon.

#WhatYouNeed

- ☞ Scarves
- ☞ Streamers or balloons
- ☞ A bedsheet or a comforter
- ☞ Some miniature vehicles
- ☞ A cardboard box
- ☞ Paper plates
- ☞ Markers, tape, glue

#HowtoPrep

- ✸ Find a table your child can crawl under and throw the comforter or the bedsheet on top to make it an enclosed space.
- ✸ On the underside of the table, hang the scarves, balloons and streamers to simulate a car wash.
- ✸ If you do not have toy cars and trucks at home, make some using a cardboard box. Cut it open from the top and draw an S on both sides; now cut along the S to resemble the wave design of a sports car. Place a paper plate as steering wheel. Now place paper plate wheels on all four sides. You can have your child paint or colour them before you stick

them on the car. Ensure your child fits inside the car from the opening on the top.

✳ Your child can also paint the outside of the cardboard car in any colour or make up a number plate as he desires. He can create a cut-out door as well.

✳ Research on the car washes prior to doing this activity.

#HowtoPlay

✳ Once your car is all set to get washed, put your child in the car and let him slide himself through the other side (or you can assist him by pushing the car, if your child is unable to).

✳ If you are using miniature cars, you can also keep a spray pump of water and while the cars are going through the tunnel, spray them with water. Let your child also go through the tunnel pretending to be a vehicle himself! Don't forget to spray him too and watch him laugh and run through the car wash.

#KeySkills

☞ Sensory exploration skills
☞ Gross motor skills
☞ Practical application skills

13. FAIRY GARDEN

Do not skip this activity if you a have a son—boys and girls love fairyland equally. A fairy garden is a miniature garden complete with a home that is usually arranged in a potted plant, designed to lure fairies, who, it is widely believed, will bring good luck and magic to your home.

#WhatYouNeed

- Any item that can be used to decorate fairyland: angel statues or miniature fairy figurines, fairy lights, small pots, piggy banks in the shape of a house or a tree, miniature lanterns, stuffed animals, small figures that your child may have made when they were younger, anything with glitter, marbles, pebbles, rocks, etc.
- A large flower pot
- Seeds of any kind and gardening materials
- Glitter

#HowtoPrep

- If you have a balcony or a ledge where you keep your plants, place a large pot filled with soil there. Plant a few seeds in it so that it is partially filled with foliage. Ensure that there is ample space left in the pot for your child to make a home for the fairies. You can have your child paint the pot and write his name on it as well.
- You can decorate this as your fairy garden. You can place little decorative structures, make a path in the pot for the fairies with pebbles, rocks, shells or marbles; you can ask

your child to use little wooden blocks to create a house or a tower for the fairies.

* You can decorate it with knick-knacks you may have at home to make it beautiful. You can create little stools and ladders, and build a bridge if the pot is large enough. Ask your child what they want their fairy garden to look like and ask them to go fetch the materials for it.

* If you have miniature animal figures, you can place them in there as well.

* You may use a bonsai tree or a tiny moon cactus plant to decorate it as well.

* Do not forget to spray it with magic dust (glitter) to entice the fairies.

#HowtoPlay

* The whole point of creating the fairy garden is to watch it grow, look out for fairies daily and hope for magical things to occur. When children go looking for magic, it happens! So, let them believe there are fairies outside their window, who are looking out for them. Ensure they take good care of their fairy garden by checking on it daily, watering the plants and making sure there is always magic dust and water for the fairies.

#KeySkills

☞ Creativity and imagination skills
☞ Adaptability skills
☞ Collaboration skills
☞ Visual comprehension skills

14. SANTA'S WORKSHOP

Anything that spells Christmas is sure to put everyone in a good mood. This activity is so much fun. It can be tailor-made to your child's interests and should be done in the days leading up to Christmas.

#WhatYouNeed

- Christmas décor
- Red and green sheets of paper
- Tables and chairs
- Craft supplies such as glue, tape, water colours, scissors, artist palette, paint brushes, water bowls, etc.
- Gift-wrapping paper, bowls, boxes, etc.
- Blocks, Legos, wooden blocks, foam blocks, Jenga blocks.

#HowtoPrep

* The important thing is to get Christmas décor. If you have a Christmas tree, put it up; spread some cotton around for snow, put the holly branch on the door; draw and paint brick walls on a sheet of paper, put that up on the walls; if you have reindeer figurines—put those up too. If you have poles around the house, you can cover them in candy stripes using red and green paper sheets. Anything you can find in the house that can be used as Christmas décor is great.

* If you can get your child in the Christmas spirit by getting him to wear the elf costume or by simply donning a hat or putting up some fairy lights, half the battle is won.

* Set up some tables that will function as stations based on your child's interest. One can be a Lego or Duplo station where you can assemble some Legos into jars or boxes. Another station can be for Magna-tiles or soft blocks or Jenga blocks. You can also set up a craft table where you can paint some rocks. You can cut-out and colour drawings of Santa Claus, a Christmas tree or snowflakes on paper plates and use them as decoration.

* One station must be the Christmas card station, where you can keep a bunch of pre-printed Christmas postcards on which your child can write. Ensure that each station is adequately stocked with paint, glue, scissors, tape, etc. You may even create an ornament station where you can place several old artificial ornaments, which can be painted or initialled.

* Finally, the last station can be the gift-packaging station, which must be stocked with gift-wrapping paper, small boxes, bags, tags, etc.

#HowtoPlay

* Have everyone from your family come into Santa's workshop one by one and let them explore it. Extol the child on the wonderful décor and the amazing workshop with its many stations.

* Your child will be Santa's elf or helper who manages each station and helps you make the toys and subsequently package, wrap and finalize them for distribution.

✳ He must personally supervise work at each station, ensure quality check and finally before gift packaging, you must seek his approval on quality.

✳ Spend some time on each activity and get your child involved by saying things like, 'I don't know how to do this. Can you help me?' or 'How do I cut this snowflake?' or 'Can you help me gift-wrap this and write my name on it?' This is so that he can help you and feel like he is in control of running the workshop as the chief elf.

✳ Finally, when all the gifts are packaged, you will have to wait to open them on Christmas when they are placed under the tree.

#KeySkills

➪ Creative thinking and imagination skills
➪ Motor skill development
➪ Vocabulary and language development
➪ Process development skills
➪ Problem-solving skills

15. PERFUME FACTORY

Children are always fascinated with the enticing aroma of perfumes and the fact that adults use them. So what could be better than to help them make their very own perfume!

#WhatYouNeed

- ᐅ Different sizes of see-through bottles and jars, preferably with pumps
- ᐅ Liquid soap dispensers
- ᐅ Ice-cream sticks or bar stirrers
- ᐅ A pair of ice-bucket tongs
- ᐅ Some food colouring
- ᐅ Fragrant oil
- ᐅ Mixing bowls
- ᐅ Test tubes and droppers (optional)
- ᐅ Aprons and goggles

#HowtoPrep

✳ Set up a station in the open, preferably on a terrace or in a garden where the children can make a mess and have access to some plants.

✳ Set up various mixing bowls, test tubes, droppers, bowls and jugs of water, food colouring, sticks, oil, etc.

#HowtoPlay

✳ Let your child unleash his creativity by mixing in pieces of plant leaves and flower petals, a drop of food colouring and a dash of liquid soap into his perfume. If the flowers are not scented, you can add a drop of the fragrant oil, and voila! You have a perfume that is safe for your child to use and enjoy. Put it into a spray pump dispenser and it will find a permanent place on your child's table in his room and will remind him of the fact that he created his own perfume.

✸ You can even go as far as labelling it with a great name and making a few extra ones to gift friends and family.

#KeySkills

☞ Hand-eye coordination skills
☞ Motor skills
☞ Creative thinking skills

16. YOGA DICE

Yoga is the easiest way to introduce the concept of physical fitness to your young one. We have to get started and get moving early!

#WhatYouNeed

☞ Yoga mats
☞ Music
☞ A few sheets of paper
☞ Colour pencils or crayons
☞ Workout gear
☞ Cardboard (optional)

#HowtoPrep

✸ Teach your child some simple animal yoga asanas—dog pose, cat pose, bear walk, crocodile pose, snake pose, mouse pose, to name a few. You can even ask your child to make sounds of the respective animal as he does the animal pose to make the learning easier and more fun.

- Once he has understood and practised the poses, help him draw them out and colour each one. You can also take print-outs and have your child write the names of the poses.

#HowtoPlay

- The yoga instructor—your child—decides what time the class is scheduled and checks your name on his clipboard before you enter the class. So, get your workout gear and lay out your mat.
- There are two ways to do this—one is to stick all the pictures on a wall and have the yoga class once a week where your child can train you to do all the poses shown in the images on the wall, or maybe more, as he is the yoga instructor. Choose a song you both like and get going! Involve other family members in the house including your nanny. This is fun for everyone and the best part—getting some workout done in the process. Always end with a freestyle dance.
- If your child is over five years of age, you can also ask him to make up a story with all the animal poses and go through the poses in the sequence of the story. This takes a little practise, but can be extremely engaging for his creative and imagination skills.
- The second way to do this activity is to create a Yoga Dice game. This is a lot of fun! Take some cardboard and create

a cube (24 inch). On each side of the six-sided cube, paste images of three poses so that it gives you a total of eighteen poses in all. Every time you roll the dice, you have to do the poses that show up and hold for one minute. Whoever can hold the poses the longest, wins!

✳ The yoga instructor announces who wins and sets goals for those who did not win, to try harder in the next week.

#KeySkills

- ☞ Focus and self-awareness
- ☞ Stress management skills
- ☞ Competitive and collaborative skills
- ☞ Communication skills
- ☞ Self-confidence and leadership skills

17. PARKING GARAGE

This one also works as a DIY storage idea (yes mommies, you can park the toy cars in here) and is great fun to make.

#WhatYouNeed

- ☞ Toilet paper rolls (around twenty)
- ☞ Water colours
- ☞ Glue
- ☞ A box or a crate

- ☞ Toy cars (around twenty)
- ☞ Markers

#HowtoPrep

- ✶ Paint all the cardboard toilet rolls in different colours (your child can try and match the colours to the colours of the toy cars you have at hand).
- ✶ Once dry, glue them one on top of the other in the crate or cardboard box.
- ✶ Ask your child to take a marker and number all the toilet paper rolls from 1–20 or 1–30, however many fit in rows in the crate or box.
- ✶ Take a marker and ask your child to write 'PARKING GARAGE K' (use the first letter of your child's name) on a sheet and stick it with tape on the top of the crate.

#HowtoPlay

- ✶ You can now call out a number between 1–30 and your child has to locate the cars of corresponding colours and park it in that garage slot.
- ✶ Your child now has a space to park all his cars and it can be dismantled as easily as it was made.

#KeySkills

- ☞ Sorting and sequencing skills
- ☞ Fine and gross motor skills
- ☞ Cognitive development skills

CHAPTER 4

#KidpreneursInTheMaking

Necessity may be the mother of invention,
but play is certainly the father.
—ROGER VON OECH

This chapter explores pretend play opportunities that mimic real-life careers and give children an opportunity to pretend to be adults. They can also earn a small allowance by doing some of these activities. Use these activities to teach various denominations of currency and to reinforce the concept that studying in school will lead them to get a job they enjoy, from which they can make money to buy things they need and want. These activities are ideal for the age group of four to eight years.

1. GROCERY STORE

A trip to the grocery store with a child can be quite daunting because they want everything! How about you create one at home for them so they can understand the mechanism of buying and selling?

#WhatYouNeed

☞ Packaged items from your kitchen such as biscuit packets, packaged flour, butter bars, sugar, cheese, yogurt, noodle packets, cans of jalapeños or olives, chocolate bars, cereal boxes, sauces, condiments, tea sachets, egg crates, almonds, packets of chips, granola bars, smoothie bottles and bathroom essentials such as toilet paper, toothpaste, etc.

☞ A calculator or a toy cash register

☞ A table or a layered organizer

☞ Paper or cloth bags

☞ A notepad and a pen

#HowtoPrep

✷ Discuss with your child the various items you find at the grocery store and show him where the Market Retail Price (MRP) is listed. On your next trip to the grocery store, ask him to help you with the price of each item so he understands how to read the pricing and check out each item later at the counter.

✷ At home, for your pretend grocery store, take your toy cash register or calculator and place a notepad and a pen next to it.

✷ Set up your toy organizer or table with the various items from your pantry or kitchen. Label the sections as Dairy, Frozen Food, Snacks, Drinks, Candies, Cooking Items, Bathroom Essentials, etc. and group the items accordingly. Keep grocery bags handy.

✳ If your child is older or has an advanced understanding of numbers, you can also write things like 'Buy 1, Get 1' or '50% Off' on coupons and hand them out at the entrance.

#HowtoPlay

✳ Invite family members and friends to your grocery store to shop.

✳ Give them their coupons and let them look around. If they ask your child for the price, tell him to give them the MRP written on the product.

✳ Once they buy groceries, bag the items and give them a bill (a sheet with the items and prices listed), and don't forget to ask your family members to give your child the money for the groceries!

✳ This is a really good activity for sharpening their maths. They end up practising addition, subtraction, multiplication and percentages without realizing it's a maths refresher because they enjoyed doing it so much.

#KeySkills

☞ Creativity and imagination skills
☞ Logical reasoning skills
☞ Practical application skills
☞ Critical thinking skills

2. DOUGHNUT SHOP

There are rarely any kids who do not love a good ol' doughnut. Let us use that to build good vocabulary, particularly descriptive adjectives, along with some mathematical skills.

#WhatYouNeed

- ☞ Cardboard
- ☞ Paper
- ☞ Paints
- ☞ Markers
- ☞ Thin cardboard boxes or paper bags
- ☞ Cash register or a calculator and a cash box

#HowtoPrep

✸ Make a menu board with a list of all kinds of doughnuts and their respective costs. Ensure that in making the menu, you describe each doughnut as if it were an advertisement for it. Ask your child to use descriptive words and colourful adjectives. Do not worry if the menu become lengthy.

✸ Take the cardboard and cut out doughnut shapes with holes in the middle. Paint different toppings for each one—sprinkles, chocolate chips, delectable cream, marshmallows, etc.

✸ Keep all the doughnuts on display and line up paper bags, or pizza or donut boxes on the table for take-away orders. Keep your cash box or register (or a calculator) handy for taking orders.

✷ You may even decorate the fascia—the signboard—and name the store. Feel free to decorate inside the store as well.

#HowtoPlay

✷ As you go into the pretend doughnut store, ensure that you ask your child various questions about the flavours of each doughnut to get your child to describe them in his own words and increase his verbal inventory of adjectives.

✷ Pay for your purchase and ensure you get some napkins along with the doughnuts.

✷ Do not forget to tell him how delicious the doughnuts were (use descriptive words here) and how happy you are with his services.

#KeySkills

☞ Creativity and imagination skills
☞ Vocabulary and language enhancement skills
☞ Sorting and sequencing skills

3. CHEF'S KITCHEN

This chocolate fudge ball no-bake recipe is so easy and foolproof that it makes every child feel like a chef. So, do not help them to make it; simply instruct, oversee and make enough so that he can share the fruits of his labour with friends and family.

#WhatYouNeed

- ☞ Chef's hat, aprons, white shirts
- ☞ ¼ cup cocoa powder (sweetened or unsweetened)
- ☞ 15 digestive biscuits
- ☞ ½ cup brown sugar (you can use dates too)
- ☞ 1 tsp vanilla extract
- ☞ ½ cup milk
- ☞ 5 tsp butter
- ☞ 4–5 almonds or walnuts
- ☞ Kitchen station
- ☞ A paper and a pen

#HowtoPlay

- ✹ Tell your child how things function in a professional kitchen. Tell him he is the chef and you are the sous chef, his assistant, so you are only there to help him. Make name tags for yourselves. Create the ambience of a professional kitchen by wearing matching chef hats and white shirts or aprons, if possible.
- ✹ Then start on the chocolate fudge balls recipe.
- ✹ Blitz the biscuits in a blender but do not make too fine a powder. Do the same for the almonds or walnuts.
- ✹ Mix the butter, vanilla extract and brown sugar till it forms a creamy base. Then add in the milk and the cocoa powder.
- ✹ Mix in the biscuits and the almonds or walnuts. Do not add water. The mixture must be thick and you should be able to roll them into balls.

✳ Once you have done that, place the balls on a tray and refrigerate for as long as you can. You can also eat them right away. Ask your child to serve them in bowls in a tray to his friends, family members, neighbours, etc.

✳ Make sure you praise him for the effort and encourage him to try something new next time.

#KeySkills

🖝 Creativity and imagination skills
🖝 Logical thinking skills
🖝 Sensory motor skills

4. POSTMAN'S MAIL SORTER

This one is another favourite! It is one that my son and I enjoy during long holidays from school where he ends up writing so many letters to his classmates, who in turn enjoy receiving them!

#WhatYouNeed

🖝 2 red chart paper sheets
🖝 3 sheets of A4-sized white paper
🖝 Tape
🖝 Glue
🖝 A calculator
🖝 A notebook or a notepad

- ☞ Pencils
- ☞ Envelopes
- ☞ A small box or a shoebox (optional)
- ☞ A bicycle or a kid's scooter (optional)
- ☞ A helmet or a cap (optional)
- ☞ A backpack or a satchel (optional)

#HowtoPrep

✸ Cut a strip of approximately 10 x 40 inches from the red chart paper. Using tape and white paper, make four pockets—taped from three sides and open on top; paste these on the red chart paper. Write your child's name on the red chart: POSTMAN VAIBHAV'S MAIL RACK. You can put your child's name on the first pocket, PARENTS on second, GRANDPARENTS on third and FRIENDS on fourth.

✸ Paste or hang this contraption wherever you want in your child's room at his eye level—behind a door, on the side of a table—or anywhere he wants it.

✸ Next, place a few pencils, a notepad and a calculator (or a pretend cashier machine if you have one at home) along with some A-5 sized sheets of papers in a stationery box or tray.

✸ Take a shoebox and cover it with red paper. Create a slot in the front with a paper cutter, so an envelope can slip through. Write the words 'POSTBOX' on the front and you can ask your child to decorate it if he so pleases. Place the postbox near the calculator and the notepad.

✹ Next, cut 1-inch squares as stamps and ask your child to make and colour any face or shape on each and keep them in the tray. If you have stamps at home, you can use those as well.

#HowtoPlay

✹ Ask each person in the family to come forward, pick a sheet of paper, write a letter or draw something on it, put it in the envelope, then buy a stamp and give it to the postman to glue it onto the envelope. The child should be encouraged to write a letter (he may draw in it too) to each of his family members and friends too.

✹ If your child can write, he may write on the envelope the names and addresses of people to whom each member wants to post the letter. Once it is done, the postman should put the letters into the correct pocket in the mail sorter (parents or friends).

✹ Once everyone has posted their letters in the mail sorter, the postman takes them out of there, puts them into an envelope and then puts the envelope into the postbox. Once there are sufficient letters in the postbox, the child can take them out and put them in his satchel or backpack and get on his scooter, wear his helmet and roam around the house delivering the letters!

✹ Also, another fun thing to do is to ask your child to keep a letter ready for any of his family members in the morning. He may draw or write in the letter, put it in an envelope, write the family member's name on it, stamp it and keep it in the respective slot. Now when the family members spot the letter in the slot during the day, they can stop to collect it!

✴ It is imperative to read up about the job responsibilities of a postman—how mail is sorted, stamped, addresses searched and the various options of sending mail through courier, flight, etc. Discussion about stamps and their associated costs based on distance, how addresses ought to be written, etc. can take place before you begin.

✴ If your child writes letters to his school friends, it is a good idea to take him to the post office and actually post them after a few days of keeping them in the FRIENDS pocket in the mail sorter. Once the recipients get their letters, ensure that your child is aware of it.

#KeySkills

- ☞ Fine motor skills
- ☞ Writing skills
- ☞ Creative thinking and imagination
- ☞ Visual processing skills
- ☞ Object recognition skills

5. SHOPPING CART

If your child is in the age group of two to six years, this activity is easy and a great deal of fun. It aids object recognition and helps with recognition of food groups and categories. This is one we had so much fun with that we developed a product out of it!

#WhatYouNeed

- Paper
- Pens
- Colour pencils or crayons or paint
- Cardboard
- Tape or glue

#HowtoPrep

* Use a thick cardboard to make a shopping cart—two long sides and two short sides along a base. Use glue or tape to put it together so it can stand on its own. It does not need wheels; just ensure that the four sides where the wheels would be are cut out in the square shapes, thereby allowing it to stand.

* Now make four shopping lists with corresponding images and names of the categories—Dairy, Vegetables, Fruits and Snacks.

* Choose any four recipes and make recipe cards with images of ingredients needed. If you're making popsicles—you will need to draw or print images of bananas, milk, honey, yogurt and popsicle moulds.

✳ Next, draw the images of all the ingredients (from the recipe cards) and the items from the shopping lists on 2x2 inch paper cut-outs, which can serve as tokens. You may also print them out and then cut them in the size of a small token.

#HowtoPlay

✳ The idea is to collect as many tokens as possible and as quickly as possible. Each player gets a recipe card and a shopping list. They have to race to fill their carts with the items on their list. When they are done, they need to take the next list and continue till they have collected all the tokens corresponding to each shopping list.

✳ If you have all the items in the lists at home (fruits, vegetables, dry fruits, snacks, etc.) you can also spread them out on a table or on a mat on the floor.

#KeySkills

☞ Visual processing skills
☞ Object recognition skills
☞ Logical reasoning skills
☞ Memory skills

6. VEGETABLE SUPERMARKET

When you have a fully stocked kitchen, this is the best activity to teach your child purchase-power, a deeper understanding of money and the process of exchanging money for things one needs.

#WhatYouNeed

- ☞ Organizer boxes that you may have at home
- ☞ Lego or magna-tiles or any building blocks
- ☞ One carton or box
- ☞ Vegetables and fruits
- ☞ Water colours
- ☞ Shopping basket or a bucket
- ☞ A kitchen weighing scale (optional)

#HowtoPrep

- ✸ Use your child's toy storage organizers that can be opened from the front to place your fruits. Segregate the fruits and vegetables first—teaching the names of each fruit and vegetable.
- ✸ Use all the blocks you can get your hands on to make an enclosure that is closed on three sides and open on top. Place the organizers with the fruits and vegetables in here.
- ✸ Take the carton and paint it in any colour your child likes. Cut it open from one side and let your child sit inside it.
- ✸ Now, make a cashier's counter. Put your child's table on the other side of the room. Write the words 'Cashier—PAY HERE' on a paper and stick it at the front of the table.
- ✸ On a side table, next to the cashier's counter, place a few sheets of paper that would make for a bill book. Place a cash box and the shopping baskets here as well.
- ✸ Set the fruits and vegetables like they are set in a supermarket with the organizers stacked next to each other in rows.

#HowtoPlay

✳ With your child's help, write down the cost of the vegetables and the fruits as per 1 kg, 500 gm, 200 gm, 100 gm (or less, depending on the amount of fruits and vegetables you have). Place this list at the cashier counter along with the bill book, a pen and other items. Also keep a calculator here.

✳ One by one, have your family members enter and explore the supermarket. They can pick up a shopping basket and start shopping with your child's assistance. They can request him to put in 100 gm of carrots, 200 gm of onions, 500 gm of oranges, 1000 grams or 1 kg of potatoes and so on. He will need to weigh each one on the scale and place them in the shopping bag.

✳ Your child will also need to add up the cost after weighing the vegetables (with your assistance) and prepare the bill accordingly. Purchasers must pay for their products before leaving.

✳ Ask your child to point out the names of vegetables and fruits, their colours and their shapes while making the bill. Use realistic pricing so your child is aware of the actual price of the produce in the market. If your child is old enough to have negotiating skills (most children master this art from the time they learn to speak), family members can try to negotiate the price. See the response of your child to such negotiations.

#KeySkills

#KeySkills

- Social and emotional development
- Organizational and planning skills
- Cognitive and memory skills
- Logical reasoning skills

7. WEATHER-WEATHER ON THE WALL

Discussing the weather is always considered the last resort when people run out of interesting things to talk about! How about making discussions on weather more interesting and productive? What better way can there be to teach your child about the weather than pretend playing the WeatherMan or WeatherWoman!

#WhatYouNeed

- A printed map of the world
- A jacket or a blazer
- A pair of sunglasses and a hat
- An umbrella
- Windcheater
- A pen or a long stick to use as a pointer

#HowtoPrep

✱ Read up on the continents and countries of the world; discuss this with your child using either the map of the world or the globe; do this for a few weeks before starting this activity. It is best to do this activity when they are being taught the same topic at school.

* Explain to him how different continents have different climates, the concept of solstices, how seasons change, what is meant by weather, and so on.

#HowtoPlay

* Once your child has understood the concept of weather and familiarized himself with the various countries and continents, stick the world map somewhere in his line of sight. It sometimes helps to put stickers of the national animal or the flag on the respective countries on the map so they can make the association.

* Get a pointer or a stick to get started. Let your child tell you about the climate in a specific country. So, if it is January, he would have to think about which season would that country have that month of the year.

* Allow him to improvise—he may feel like assessing the severity of the winter in a country or the rains elsewhere, etc. This will help him to put to use some good words and phrases.

* He may also change his clothes or put on sunglasses, a hat, hold an umbrella or wear a windcheater for dramatic effect as he is presenting the weather report. Sit back and engage with your child in a fun performance of the Weatherman!

#KeySkills

☞ Vocabulary enhancement and language development

↳ Logical reasoning skills
↳ Visual recognition skills
↳ Correlation and purposeful thinking skills
↳ Problem-solving skills

8. VISIT TO THE ART GALLERY

A DIY art gallery auction is one of my personal favourites. You must do this one when you have a bunch of family or friends coming over. Select a theme together for your little one to unleash his inner Picasso and once his collection is ready, host an art auction!

#WhatYouNeed

↳ Many sheets of paper
↳ Art supplies such as water colours, crayons, colour pencils, colour pens, etc.
↳ Craft supplies such as pom-poms, sponges, shredded paper, threads, crushed chalk
↳ Post-its
↳ An easel (optional)
↳ Strings or ribbons (optional)
↳ Clips (optional)

#HowtoPrep

✳ Set up an easel with art papers. Tell your child that he is putting up an art show in a few days and as the artist, he has to paint or draw using a specific theme or concept (different scenarios like a picnic; humans or animals; raw or cooked food; places like a farm; things, like a postbox, are some examples). He needs to use different kinds of art papers, use paints for one, colour pencils for another, crayons for the next, and so on. He also needs to create something using craft supplies.

✳ Pull out old art-and-craft pieces your child may have made over the last few months either in school or at home. If you have smaller paintings that your child has done in a class or school, you can tie a string from one side of the room to the other and using clips, hang up the art pieces on the string.

✳ Alternatively, you may stick them on the windows or on the walls of any one room in your house.

✳ Tell your child to fix a time for the art exhibition and create an invitation where he has to give a name to his collection. For example, 'Kiaan Invites You to His Art Exhibition named *Beach Life* at 6 PM, Thursday, August 5'.

#HowtoPlay

✳ Ask your child to distribute the invitations to the family members and friends he wishes to invite.

✻ Then, at the scheduled time, he has to take the family and friends group to his exhibition where he needs to walk them to each painting and explain his inspiration and the concept behind it.

✻ Once he is done with the explanations, he can give the group Post-it notes on which they can give his work stars (either four or five stars, not less) to help boost the child's confidence. They can also give feedback on which paintings they liked the best.

✻ People can also place bids to buy the paintings and fight each other for them to make it fun for the child. Family members can finally choose to purchase one painting each and give the child a small token amount (in both bills and coins). This will also help the child understand the various denominations of currency.

✻ When all your child's works are sold, it will do wonders for his confidence and he will be encouraged to draw, paint and create new works of art, and also to experiment with unconventional materials as well.

✻ While setting up the art auction room, discuss with your child how an art gallery functions, how a bid works, the pricing and range; also discuss ascending and descending numbers while bidding.

✻ Engage in a discussion on the various concepts the child has attempted to illustrate. Ask related questions like: Are you drawing a farm? Who all are on the farm? Which animals do you find there? Who is the caretaker of the farm? What does the farmer wear? These questions will help fuel his imagination and assist him in bringing a more realistic perspective to his paintings.

#KeySkills

- Creative thinking and imagination skills
- Visual processing skills
- Purposeful discussion skills
- Organizational and planning skills

9. DIY COFFEE SHOP

This one has stuck and is kind of permanent in our house. Every Sunday at 4 p.m., our son becomes the coffee shop vendor and screams out for us to meet him at the bar. Clad in his chef outfit, complete with the hat, he assumes the avatar of a coffee shop owner and even has vivid conversations with us about how well his coffee shop is doing! This is a great pretend play activity to build vocabulary skills and increase your child's comprehension.

#WhatYouNeed

- If you have a high table or a bar at home, this activity is easy to do. If not, use any table and a couple of stools or chairs.
- An assortment of bakes—cupcakes, cakes, scones, croissants, breads

- Cups, saucers, spoons, knives
- Sugar sachets
- Two thermoses
- A coffee machine and coffee powder
- Milk
- Cocoa powder
- Biscuits
- A blackboard and some chalks
- A notebook and a pen

#HowtoPrep

* First, have a discussion with your child about the coffee shop as a business model—how one makes money while selling coffee. Explain to your child that if the coffee costs him Rs 2, he has to price it at Rs 4 to his customers so that he makes a profit and that is how a successful business works. Then, discuss the creative and technical side of it— how he needs to practise how to mix three basic things together to create a cup of tea or coffee or hot chocolate.

* Spread out a tablecloth on the table (if it is a high table, even better)

* Keep some stools around the table.

* Spread a scrumptious array of desserts (real and pretend).

* Mommy or Daddy can pre-make black coffee (or black tea) and keep it ready in a thermos, along with some sugar, tea sachets, cocoa powder, coffee stencils (if you use them), milk, coffee mugs and saucers.

✱ If you use a coffee machine at home, plug it in and keep it at the bar.

✱ On the blackboard, encourage your child to put up a menu and price the products accordingly. For example, a latte should be more expensive than plain milk, and a slice of bread would be cheaper than a dessert. Encourage him to use whole numbers for the pricing and keep the amount nominal.

✱ Your child can also create a logo for the coffee shop by cutting up different pieces of paper and placing them on the bar in the shape of a coffee mug or by using glitter and other craft accessories. Encourage your child to name his coffee shop and spend some time thinking about a name that is meaningful to him. He may use his own name or something that simply reflects a mood like 'Happiness Coffee Shop'. This is the first step in your child's life of creating a brand of his own and understanding a little bit of entrepreneurship. Tell your child the name must be catchy and should resonate with customers. Encourage whatever he comes up with.

✱ You can help him to add aesthetic elements to his coffee shop such as fairy lights, candles, flowers, or anything else that one would find in a coffee shop.

#HowtoPlay

✱ Once it is set up, your child can invite family members and friends to come to the coffee shop at a stipulated time.

* When someone comes by the coffee shop, tell your child to ask them to take a seat, point them in the direction of the blackboard menu and ask what they would like.

* If they order a tea or a coffee, ask your to child make it (by adding milk and sugar to the pre-made black tea or coffee from the thermos) and serve it to his customer. Once he gets the hang of it, he can do it by himself (under his parent's vigilant and supervising eye).

* Hot chocolate can be made easily by simply mixing the cocoa powder with some sugar and milk, and your child can also enjoy the drink with you.

* Your child can also offer you a dessert or a slice of bread along with your beverage.

* Once you have enjoyed your beverage, you can ask for the bill.

* Your child now has to compute the bill and charge you for the items consumed. He needs to write down the number in his notebook, tear the sheet and give it to you as a bill.

* Once you receive the bill, you can correct it if there is any discrepancy.

* If your child has a theatrical bent of mind, remind your child that he must assume the role of the coffee shop owner the entire time and not break character. So, all the conversations you have, can be around coffee, tea, other customers, items that sold out quickly that morning, etc. Superheroes and imaginary people may also be brought up as customers! Believe everything and play along. Encourage the make-believe conversations.

✷ Remember never to leave the coffee shop without saying that it was the best coffee shop you have ever been to! Reinforcement is everything.

#KeySkills

- Motor skill development
- Cognitive skill development
- Creative thinking skills
- Language and vocabulary development

10. CANDY STORE/ICE-CREAM SHOP

When you have a party and have guests coming over, you can set up a remarkable and delectable dessert table, but isn't it more fun to involve your children and set up a DIY ice-cream stand or a candy store instead? All it takes is a little bit of planning and a few items and your child won't stop smiling.

#WhatYouNeed

- A chest of drawers or an organizer with buckets
- Cardboard sheets
- A colourful fabric
- Ice-cream tubs

- ➣ Ice-cream scooper
- ➣ Bowls
- ➣ Small jars or bowls for candy
- ➣ Candies of different colours
- ➣ Blackboard
- ➣ Paper and pens for signage
- ➣ Weighing machine

#HowtoPrep

✴ Take a large chest of drawers or an organizer; use cardboard to build two stands on top of it. Now make an awning to rest on these stands using a coloured fabric. You can also create a signpost for the ice-cream shop or the candy store and hang it to the awning fabric.

✴ You must also have a menu written on a blackboard or whiteboard, with the pricing.

✴ Set up the ice-cream tubs next to each other along with the scoopers, spoons and bowls. If you have a lot of people coming, then put the ice creams in an ice box on top of the organizer.

✴ Fill up jars with different kinds of candies and set them next to each other. Keep some paper bowls handy so your customers can put their candies in them.

#HowtoPlay

✴ When your guests come home, tell them that this time the dessert stall is being managed by your child. You can price the desserts a nominal amount or provide play money to your guests to pay for the ice creams and candies to encourage the child.

✳ Based on the choice of the customer, a scoop can be taken out using the scooper and placed in the bowl and handed over.

✳ For the candies, allow the customer to pick the candies and place them in their paper bowls. Then let your child weigh them on the weighing scale and charge them as he has planned.

✳ This activity is so much fun for children because it allows them to act like the responsible adult and the manager of the stall. It allows them to pretend to be running a business. The money (real or play) is just an incentive to encourage them in their effort.

#KeySkills

☞ Gross motor skills
☞ Creative thinking skils
☞ Practical application of concepts
☞ Sequencing and sorting skills
☞ Visual comprehension skills

11. FLOWER STAND

This one is a work of art in the making and the best part is that the prep for this takes a while. So plan to do this on a weekend and spend the whole week prepping for it.

#WhatYouNeed

- ☞ Jars that can work as flowerpots—yogurt cartons or vases that are not made of glass
- ☞ Felt fabric
- ☞ Scissors, tape and glue
- ☞ Craft supplies such as string, ribbons, forks, pom-poms, cotton, cloth, pipe cleaners, pencils, thermocol balls, paper, pens, paint, etc.
- ☞ Salt, rice
- ☞ Cash register or cash box
- ☞ Seeds and pots

#HowtoPrep

- ✷ Cover the cartons or pots in felt or chart paper and get them ready for planting.
- ✷ You can put cotton, salt or rice or anything that can hold flowers, inside the pot.
- ✷ You can make the flowers out of literally anything you have at home. For instance, you can use a fork and paint the top-part pink and the bottom green and attach a painted leaf to it to make a tulip. You can attach thermocol balls to the pipe cleaners to make them look like lilacs; strips of fabric in different colours can be tied to a pencil to make pretend poppies or lilies. You can use pom-pom balls to make sunflowers. Even pistachio shells can be used as accessories to make flowers, or you may use your child's handprints or fingerprints arranged in the shape of a flower. You can cut and stick them to a straw to form a flower.

✳ Display your flowerpots and label them with the flower names and if possible, do add price tags as well. Finding writing opportunities in every activity is always a brownie point.

✳ It would be great to also pot your own plants with whatever seeds you have available at home and once they have sprouted a little, add them to your collection for the Sunday flower stand.

✳ Keep a cash register or a cash box at the ready.

#HowtoPlay

✳ Show your child pictures or read a book about the various flowers of the world, where they come from and what they are known for.

✳ Once he has an understanding of the flowers, set out to make your flower stand.

✳ Get the stand ready and set up your flowerpots. You can even add in real flowerpots and await your customers' reactions.

✳ Ask your friends or family members to come to your flower stand, describe your flowerpots to them and charge a nominal amount for your flowers.

#KeySkills

☞ Motor skills
☞ Boosts language development and vocabulary
☞ Increased emotional and social awareness
☞ Object recognition skills
☞ Memory skills

12. CANDLE MAKING

Want your child to learn the basics of entrepreneurship early? Rule number 1: It is hard work. Nothing like making and packaging candles to show your child how much effort can go into the creation of a product.

#WhatYouNeed

- ⤳ Soy wax
- ⤳ Candle wicks
- ⤳ Fragrance oil (optional)
- ⤳ A heatproof container (glass or mason)
- ⤳ Crayons of different colours and sizes
- ⤳ Glitter

#HowtoPrep

- ✳ Attach the candlewick to the bottom of the jar either by putting it on hot wax or with a double-sided tape.
- ✳ Pour the hot melted wax into the glass jar (ensure that it can withstand hot temperatures). Add a drop of your fragrance oil into the soy wax. All this is done or supervised by parents of course.
- ✳ Then take all your child's old crayons, melt them in the microwave or on the stove (you can do it colour-wise or mix them all in together) and add wax to it. Then layer the candle with this mix; keep alternating with soy wax.
- ✳ Your child can also decorate the candle with some glitter or even tie a ribbon around the jar.

✴ He can also hide small decorative items in the wax in the jar.

#HowtoPlay

✴ Your child can start his mini business by selling these wonderful candles. Ask him to get creative with the colours, the layering and the manner in which each candle is created.

✴ Ask him to add up the costs incurred to create each candle and to price them accordingly.

✴ Encourage your child's first business by displaying his candles prominently around your house, showing the candles to the people who come over, promoting them to your friends and ensuring that others in the family support him by buying them. That first feeling of selling something that one has put a lot of effort into creating is wonderful for a child. The money earned can be spent on buying something your child wants or on going out for a treat together. The important thing to emphasize is that people like the candles and so they are buying them, and not the amount of money earned. He should feel that the real accomplishment was creating something of value and not just earning a few bucks—that acknowledgement of his effort will bring him true gratification.

#KeySkills

☞ Introduction to the basics of entrepreneurship
☞ Comprehension of the economics of buying and selling
☞ Self-confidence
☞ Cognitive and reasoning skills

☞ Fine and gross motor skills
☞ Creative and imagination skills

13. LEMONADE STAND

This has been an American entrepreneurial debut for most children for decades. Do this on a day when you have friends and family coming over and involve more children in the activity. A definite by-product of this is that your child will start to then think of creative ways to use what is around him once he sees some success with this activity.

#WhatYouNeed

☞ Mint leaves, powdered sugar, fresh lemon juice, coconut water (optional), black pepper, water and salt
☞ Canisters, glasses or mason jars
☞ Lemon slices for garnish
☞ A table and a tablecloth
☞ Bill book and cash box

#HowtoPrep

✳ Explain the recipe to the children. Allow them to make the lemonade and store it in a few jugs. Remember that it is less about the product and more about the process. So, in case their lemonade does not work out, encourage them to make a strawberry banana smoothie or serve pineapple juice instead. Keep the back-up ingredients handy.

* Help the children make a lemonade stall. Decorate the stall as nicely as you can with whatever you have at home— paints, crayons, coloured paper, the works!

* If you can build a stand on top of a table using cardboard, even better! Ask your child to write the words 'LEMONADE STAND' (or 'SMOOTHIE STALL' or 'JUICE STAND') on a sheet, along with the price of the lemonade, and hang it on the stand.

* Keep your cash box and bill book ready to accept payments.

#HowtoPlay

* When your guests start to arrive, point them in the direction of your little entrepreneur's set-up.

* When the guests purchase the lemonade from your child, you will see them gleam and glow—like a true entrepreneur who has sold his first product. You'll see the look of relief, happiness and excitement.

* Allow your child to interact with customers, sell his product, raise bills and collect the money. Ask the guests to appreciate the child's effort and the drink.

#KeySkills

* Self-confidence
* Conversational skills
* Knowledge of currency denominations
* Introduction to the world of entrepreneurship

14. SHOE SHOP

Let's face it—children love their shoes. But putting their shoes on sale and not actually selling them can be most fun!

#WhatYouNeed

- An array of shoes (yours and your child's)
- Shoeboxes
- Table
- Cash register or cash box
- Paper
- Pens
- Shopping bags

#HowtoPlay

- ✳ Display all the shoes and the shoeboxes on the table and on the floor.
- ✳ Have people come in and urge them to try on the shoes and buy them. If they select a pair, have your child box it, bag it, give the customer a bill and accept the money.
- ✳ To check for size, you can use papers on which the child can trace the outline of the foot of the customer. Ask your child to match the traced size to the shoes.
- ✳ You can also use dolls, take their measurements and see if they fit into your child's shoes or ones they have outgrown. Children will have a great time doing this activity.

11. SHOE SHOP

#KeySkills

- ☞ Creative thinking and imagination skills
- ☞ Logical reasoning
- ☞ Social and emotional skills

15. PIZZA PARLOUR FUN

Who doesn't love pizza? Pizza is everything! Going to a pizza parlour and selecting your toppings is a real treat for the kids. Beware, this one is so much fun that it might be hard to shake off and you may end up doing it every weekend!

#WhatYouNeed

- ☞ A red or red-and-white chequered tablecloth
- ☞ Table
- ☞ Chairs
- ☞ Large cardboard box
- ☞ Water colours or pens or crayons
- ☞ Glue or tape
- ☞ Paper
- ☞ Felt or coloured chart paper
- ☞ A play phone
- ☞ Serving utensils—trays, cutlery, etc.
- ☞ Pizza boxes, if available

#HowtoPrep

✸ Draw on a sheet of paper several vegetables that can serve as pizza toppings, such as mushrooms, jalapeños, bell peppers, chillies, tomatoes, aubergines, pineapples, cheese, pepperoni and so on. Cut them out and put them in an open box.

✸ Cut out circles in brown, red and white felt or coloured paper, with each circle being slightly smaller than the other—the brown being the largest and the white being the smallest. These will serve as the layers of the pizza. Place these in another box.

✸ Set up your pizza table with a tablecloth and place the menu card that shows the different pizza toppings you offer. Let your child write it himself.

✸ Next to the table, set up your cardboard-box kitchen. Cut out the box in such a way so there is no top or bottom and just the four adjacent sides of the box. Paint them red and white. Name the pizza parlour after your child, for example, 'JADE'S PIZZA PARLOUR' and create a banner. You can also write your timings on the banner, like most restaurants do.

✸ Inside the kitchen, place a table on which to keep the various circular pizza cut-outs and the toppings. You may also place a rolling pin, cutlery, trays and other serving utensils there.

✸ Place a play phone or a real phone in the kitchen as well, from where your child can take take-away orders.

#HowtoPlay

* Get your child under a chef's hat and let him man the kitchen.
* Your family members and you may enter the restaurant, order different pizzas, while also placing take-away orders. Your child must handle the calls buzzing on his kitchen phone as well as the rush in the restaurant.
* Ask for different kinds of toppings to see how fast and how well he can layer the pizza. The first layer is of the brown felt which is the base, the second is the red one, which is the red sauce and the third is the white, which is the cheese, and on top of that are the various vegetable toppings.
* Watch your child pack pizza boxes and get them ready for delivery meticulously with correct labelling and bills.
* You will be surprised how this activity can be a great creative and mental stimulant for your child.
* He can also spend a lot of time playing this alone and pretending to get orders.
* To make it more fun, you can also place your orders through an order form from your bedroom and have your pizza delivered to you in style.

#KeySkills

* Creativity and imagination skills
* Social skills and emotional development
* Logical thinking skills
* Purposeful thinking
* Organizational and planning skills

16. VISIT TO THE HAIRDRESSER

Our little entrepreneurs love pretending to be adults. Giving them an insight into adult lives gives them a better understanding of life. Going to the hairdresser can be much more fun at home—if you do it right!

#WhatYouNeed

- Hairdryer
- Spray bottle filled with water
- Child-friendly pair of scissors (or a play one)
- Adult hair clips and/or rollers
- Cash box or cash register
- Notepad to function as a bill book
- Pen
- Hairbrush
- Stool
- Adult bathrobe
- Mirror
- Tip jar

#HowtoPrep

* If your child wants to play hairdresser, first decide if he wants to service his toy characters, dolls, stuffed animals or family members. All are feasible but require slightly different arrangements.

* For example, for the adults in the family, a large mirror, a stool or a chair and an adult-size bathrobe or housecoat are

required. Similarly, if it is a doll, then a small mirror, a toy stool and a hand towel or hankerchief to cover the doll is good enough.

✳ Ask your child to set up the chair in front of a mirror in the room where the hairdressing will take place. Keep the bathrobe handy.

✳ Set up the cash register, bill book and other items on a counter at the entrance of the room. Make a sign with all the services being offered—nail painting, hairstyling, hair wash, blow dry, head massage, etc. with the corresponding prices (nominal). Keep a jar that says 'TIPS' by the cash register.

✳ Set up all the hair clips, rollers and pretty hairbands as well.

#HowtoPlay

✳ Simply enter your child's room or wherever the play is set up and inform them of the service you are looking for—let us say, a head massage and a blow dry. Your child will tell you what those cost. You will need to pay for the services, take a bill and then take a seat.

✳ Your child can spray your hair with some water, and comb or brush them thoroughly. Then he may begin massaging your head and finally drying the hair (with the dryer on cold dry if your child is not used to handling it).

✳ Finally, he will style your hair with appropriate accessories as he deems fit.

✳ When he is done, tell him you are grateful for his service and that it was the best one you have had so far and leave him a tip in the tip jar.

✴ While setting up the salon, discuss the different things required to run a business—the services offered, the price, the acceptance of payment against a bill, the preparation and planning for the services offered to the clients, etc. Discuss the manner in which a business owner should speak to a client—using words like 'please', 'thank you', 'ma'am' and 'sir'.

#KeySkills

- ☞ Logical thinking skills
- ☞ Social skills and emotional development skills
- ☞ Role-play skills

17. FASHION SHOW

This is a great parent-child bonding activity to do when you are in the mood for some dress-up!

#WhatYouNeed

- ☞ A rack to hang adult clothes
- ☞ A small rack to hang your child's clothes (you can use a curtain rod or a stick and rest it between two tall chairs to create a rack for your kid)
- ☞ A mirror
- ☞ Some lights (optional)
- ☞ Make-up products
- ☞ Clothing accessories such as purses, hats, jewellery, etc.

#HowtoPrep

❋ Set up a little make-up station with a few make-up items, hair accessories, a hairbrush and a mirror.

❋ Hang some outfits that you will go in and select together for the fashion show. The important part of this activity is allowing your child to select their favourite outfits from your wardrobe and letting them pick coordinated accessories and shoes.

❋ Then lay out a carpet (even a yoga mat will do) and start the show!

#HowtoPlay

❋ Get a couple of family members to sit as the audience and get the show started!

❋ You and your child can take turns to walk the ramp in your outfits and the audience gets to vote on their favourite outfit!

❋ Finally, check which outfits got the best score and wear those for the next family dinner.

#KeySkills

☞ Social and emotional development
☞ Self-confidence
☞ Creative thinking and imagination skills
☞ Collaboration and healthy competition skills

CHAPTER 5

#CONVERSATIONBOOST

*In play, a child is always above his average age,
above his daily behaviour; in play, it is as
though he were a head taller than himself.*
—LEV VYGOTSKY

This chapter focuses on activities that have a larger conversational element and will help enhance vocabulary and language development. Ensure that you back these activities up with some research so your child can locate these activities within a larger understanding of the concept and is able to articulate his thoughts and discuss them with some kind of personal experience. These activities are ideal for children in the age group of three to seven years.

1. SPACE STATION

Imagine a control centre from where you can see the entire solar system and monitor movements and collisions of spaceships, planets, asteroids and meteors. This activity works to expose your child's imagination to the wonders of space.

#WhatYouNeed

- ☞ Chair and table
- ☞ Aluminium foil
- ☞ Books on the planets
- ☞ Paper
- ☞ Calculator or remote controls or any gadgets with buttons
- ☞ Laptop or iPad (real or play)
- ☞ Globe
- ☞ Anything that resembles a lever or a toy that has a lever and can be pushed and pulled
- ☞ Binoculars or telescope (real or play)
- ☞ String

#HowtoPrep

- ✴ Get your child to draw each planet and colour them in. They can also draw the sun, the moon, some asteroids, meteors and others rocks or cut them out of aluminium foil.
- ✴ Once done, you can string these up and hang them from a curtain rod.
- ✴ Place the globe on the table, alongside the remote controls, the calculator, the cash register, the laptop or iPad, the toy lever, the binoculars, etc. This forms your space station control centre.
- ✴ Cover the wall behind the table with aluminium foil. This will be your child's window—a control center—to check in on the other planets.

✳ You can put a sign there that says 'SPACE STATION CONTROL CENTRE'.

#HowtoPlay

✳ This is a great way to introduce your child to outer space. You must begin by researching on the solar system and the planets. Explain how gravity works in outer space, that objects simply float around rather than staying put. Tell them interesting facts about the planets and discuss other things you find in space such as asteroids, meteors, etc.

✳ Create an astronaut costume for your child using a windcheater and white pants. Ask him to make a badge for himself with his NASA credentials and his photograph and name, which he can wear around his neck.

✳ Once he is ready, he can start (pretend) looking at each planet through his binoculars. Ask him if he sees any asteroids or meteors coming his way so he can move out of their way without any collisions.

✳ He must periodically check on all the hanging planets, the sun and the moon and report his observations on other spaceships landing on these planets, if there is any form of life there, the temperature and what kind of people or animals he thinks he can see there. You will be surprised at their creativity and imagination as they can come up with wonderful stories while looking through those binoculars.

✳ This activity is better performed by two or more children.

#KeySkills

- ☞ Cognitive skills
- ☞ Logical thinking skills
- ☞ Gross motor skills
- ☞ Communication skills
- ☞ Self-direction, confidence, independence

2. CALENDAR STATION

No better way to teach your child the days of the week, the months of the year and time, than playing Calendar Station.

#WhatYouNeed

- ☞ **A board**
- ☞ **Sheets of paper**
- ☞ **Coloured chart paper**
- ☞ **Coloured pens and pencils, crayons**
- ☞ **Paper plates**
- ☞ **Cardboard**
- ☞ **Scissors and tape**
- ☞ **Calendar**

#HowtoPrep

- ✳ The prep for this takes a week and is a lot of fun, so don't rush it!

✳ Ask your child to make a 'Calendar Station' sign with your help and stick it on top of a big cardboard sheet.

✳ On one side of the cardboard, stick a calendar that has sheets for every month, which can be torn off. Make sure you ask your child to highlight every holiday in the monthly calendar. For instance, for December 25, he can draw a Christmas tree next to the date, and for his birthday, he can draw a cake, and so on.

✳ Below the calendar sheets, place a sign that says 'TODAY IS . . .' Now, use chart paper of different colours to create three envelopes that are open from the top. Stick these below the calendar.

✳ Now, make notecard inserts to go into these envelopes; the inserts should have all the days of the week from Monday to Sunday, the dates from 1 to 31 and the months from January to December written on them.

✳ Put another sign that says 'TODAY, THE WEATHER IS . . .' and below that put three envelopes. For the inserts, ask your child to create three notecards—'Cloudy and Rainy', 'Sunny', and 'Cold and Windy'.

✳ Next, put up another sign that says, 'THE TIME IS . . .' and below that, stick three envelopes with Hours, Minutes and AM/PM written on them respectively. Keep ready the notecard inserts for the hours from 1 to 12, and for the minutes, 1 to 60, in multiples of five.

✳ Let your child do all the work to get this ready even if it takes longer. You may need to help him with the tear-away sheets (you can also print these out).

✳ Keep a box of colour pencils or crayons near the Calendar Station.

#HowtoPlay

✳ Every morning your child needs to put in the notecards for the correct date, day and month in the designated envelopes. He also has to update the weather envelopes with the correct notecards. He then has to cross out the previous day on the sheet and if the month has ended, he must remove the tear-away sheet of that month. Ask him if he sees any occasions coming up in that week. If he has a play date or a birthday party coming up, he can write that in next to that date or ask him to draw something to signify the same.

✳ Reading the time is a very tedious activity for children. So getting them to like and enjoy it through this station can aid their language and comprehension skills.

#KeySkills

☞ Creative skills
☞ Logical thinking skills
☞ Cognitive and reasoning skills
☞ Numerical skills
☞ Language development skills
☞ Problem-solving skills

3. HOTEL CHECK-IN COUNTER

This one is good for building those memory skills by emulating a hotel check-in counter.

#WhatYouNeed

- A cardboard box large enough for one child to fit in
- Map of the city
- Play Phone
- Calculator or pretend cash register
- Post-It notes
- Pens, notebooks, office supplies
- Small suitcase

#HowtoPrep

- ✷ Create a reception window cut-out using a cardboard box (that your child can fit behind) and put up a sign that says 'HOTEL RECEPTION' on top of it.
- ✷ Have your child dress as a receptionist in smart, formal clothes with his hair neatly done up.
- ✷ Print a map of the city and circle some familiar places on them such as a garden, a monument, a school, a zoo, a museum, a market, a shopping mall, a restaurant, etc.
- ✷ Keep a toy phone and a cash register or a calculator, stationary organizers with Post-its, some notebooks, pens and other office supplies, inside the box next to the window cut-out. The child or adult playing the guest needs to be

dressed in appropriate clothing and carry some travel gear like a bag or a suitcase and perhaps a jacket and a hat.

#HowtoPlay

✳ This is a great activity for two or more children or a family member. Ask them to pick their favourite city from the ones they have visited or it could be the city they live in as well. And set up the pretend play hotel check-in counter there.

✳ There are two roles to be played—the receptionist and the guest(s). The receptionist has to warmly welcome the guest(s) to the hotel and then take their luggage.

✳ The guest's job is to ask a lot of questions—the tariff of the rooms, the floor the room is on, what kind of a view it has, if there is a laundry service and a swimming pool, where can they eat at the hotel, the other amenities the hotel provides, where can they go for shopping and sightseeing, which restaurants they can visit, etc.

✳ The receptionist's job is to provide all the answers with the use of the map of the city. The receptionist may receive calls during the conversation and he can feel free to answer them.

✳ If your child has travelled frequently with you, they will be able to mimic the way a receptionist or a concierge converses with the guests. For instance, my son even offered me a welcome drink because he remembered it is customary when guests arrive at a resort.

#KeySkills

- ☞ Creativity and imagination skills
- ☞ Problem-solving skills
- ☞ Cognitive application of the mind
- ☞ Memory or recall skills
- ☞ Vocabulary development skills

4. PUPPET SHOW

This is one to get those motor skills and creative juices going. And it is very easy to do!

#WhatYouNeed

- ☞ A large box
- ☞ Coloured paper
- ☞ Colour pens
- ☞ Ice-cream sticks or stirrers
- ☞ Cardboard

#HowtoPrep

- ✳ Three ways of making the puppets:
  - ✳ You can draw the animal or human characters on paper, cut them out and attach them to long sticks. Use cardboard pieces, ice-cream sticks or long stirrers from the bar for this purpose.

* You can use crepe paper for the puppet body.
* Alternatively, you can also take small paper gift bags and draw on them. Put your hand in the bag to work them.

* Now it is time to prepare the puppet theatre. Cut out the back of the cardboard box. Then, cut out a rectangle from the front side leaving a small border around it. This front will be the space/stage where the performance will take place. Leave the roof of the box open.

* Draw any scenery on a sheet of paper, like a farm, a forest or a garden. Paste/hang this scenery using tape on the back of the cardboard box to serve as the background for the puppet show. This can be removed and replaced with another scenery later.

* Cover the outside of the box with coloured paper and decorate it.

* Now draw the characters of your child's choice such as an animal, a dragon, a unicorn, etc. on paper; cut them out. Paste them on sticks and your puppets are ready.

#HowtoPlay

* Now, ask your child to stand on one side of the set-up. He may start the show by slipping the puppets from the open roof slot so they are visible against the background and tell a fantastical story!

* You can also turn the theatre around, use a torch and create a shadow puppet show!

#KeySkills

- ᕗ Language development skills
- ᕗ Vocabulary
- ᕗ Cognitive development
- ᕗ Logic and reasoning skills
- ᕗ Visual processing skills

5. TREASURE HUNT

Remember when we went treasure hunting at home as children? The excitement in looking for those chits of paper or items was unbeatable. A treasure hunt is a way of challenging the mind and thinking laterally. So, the next time your child asks for an untimely gift, organize a treasure hunt and make him 'work' for it.

#WhatYouNeed

- ᕗ Notecards and pens

#HowtoPlay

- ✳ Make a series of rhyming clues on chits of paper whose solution will be another item in another part of your house. For example, your first clue could be— 'Mommy says it is time to go get some beautiful flowers, look behind the item you use to check the hours.' Once your child has figured out that the answer is a clock, he will rush to all the clocks in your house till he finds clue number 2, which will lead him to another item in your house. Also, under the clock and the next set of items, there will be a series of letters of the alphabet, which he has to collect during the course of the treasure hunt.

✴ As your child comes to the end of the treasure hunt, he should have collected several letters. Now, he must put the letters together and unscramble them to get the last and final clue. If the letters are HINECKT, unscrambling it leads to KITCHEN, which is where his present is hidden!

✴ Try and time the treasure hunt so there is some pressure to solve the clues quickly. Involve other children or family members so they can try and solve them too. This will help your child learn healthy collaboration and competition, which also makes it more exciting and fun.

#KeySkills

☞ Creative thinking skills
☞ Critical and logical thinking skills
☞ Memory skills
☞ Cognitive skills
☞ Communication skills

6. SENSORY BIN

When we were children, there was a game we played wherein we were blindfolded and had to guess items through touch, feel and scent. There are innumerable benefits to this as it provides recognition of multiple senses and serves as a great conversation starter and a good activity to do during high conflict times such as mealtime or bath time.

#WhatYouNeed

- ☞ Go around the house and collect various items and put them in a large box or a toy storage organizer. Select items that are unconnected to each other. For instance, you could put in a Batman figurine, a jar, a pot, a pencil, a crayon, a spare doorknob, a hairbrush, a toothbrush, a watch, a ring, a sock, a tie, a bottle of perfume, a bath toy, a glove, a screwdriver, a food item, a glass, a puzzle piece, etc.
- ☞ A blindfold

#HowtoPlay

- ✱ Blindfold your child and ask him to first guess all the items by touching them.
- ✱ Once he has guessed them, all the ones he guessed correctly ought to be placed back in the bin. The ones he did not guess correctly have to be placed separately.
- ✱ Once he sees the items, he has to build a story that involves all the items. Allow your child to take a lead on this and enjoy the process of making up a story no matter how

ridiculous it may sound. In fact, the more creative, the better.

#KeySkills

- ☞ Creativity and imagination skills
- ☞ Cognitive development skills
- ☞ Visual processing skills
- ☞ Sensory motor skills

7. WORLD'S GREATEST SUPERHERO

Which child does not want to be Wonder Woman or an Avenger? Superheroes keep our imagination active and harness creativity from the deepest crevices of our minds. So, getting to train a superhero is another level of fun. You can do some or all of the tests we have outlined depending on the materials available to you.

#WhatYouNeed

- ☞ Items to make a superhero costume
- ☞ Beads and a string
- ☞ Water colours, paper, crayons
- ☞ Pom-poms
- ☞ Coloured chart paper
- ☞ Bowling pins or a dartboard
- ☞ Legos

- Blocks for an obstacle course
- Magna-tiles
- Letter tiles from Scrabble or similar board games

#HowtoPrep

* Turn your child's room into a Superhero School, where they are trained to be superheroes and their strength is tested. There will be a series of stations for the different kinds of tests to be conducted. Each test will have a signboard with its name on it.

* First is a *hand-eye coordination test*. Arrange a basket with beads on a table with a string or a ribbon.

* Second is the *dexterity test*. Stick five to six coloured paper circles on a chart paper and number each circle. Keep pom-poms of the corresponding colours in a tray next to it.

* Third is the *intelligence test*. Use Scrabble letter tiles or a lightbox (the pretty ones with the letters) and display the letters on the table so your child can make his own words using those letters.

* Fourth is the *motor skills test*. Keep some craft materials and a printed list of all the superhero logos. Your child has to copy it using the paints, crayons or using play dough.

* Fifth is the *responsiveness test*, keep a Lego station with its baseplate ready to go.

* Sixth is the *numbers test*. Keep sheets of coloured paper and put the numbers from 0 to 10 on them—the first sheet will have the number 0, the second sheet will have the

number 1, and so on. Stick them to the floor with tape in the manner of hopscotch.

✴ Seventh is the *power test*. Set up an obstacle course using blocks or any items from around the house and finally at the end of the obstacle course lay out the Magna-tiles or blocks for your child to make a tower.

✴ Eighth is the *strength test*. Set up the felt or velcro dartboard, or any other game that involves physical strength, such as bowling pins or steel cups in a pyramid and a ball.

✴ Finally, create a finish line at the end with a ribbon. Keep a handmade certificate that reads, 'You have passed the Superhero Test and you are now the WORLD'S GREATEST SUPERHERO'.

#HowtoPlay

✴ Get your child into their favourite superhero gear and costume.

✴ Then tell him that if he wants to become the world's greatest superhero, he needs to pass certain tests.

✴ Take him to the room where you have arranged the various tests.

✴ Hand-eye coordination test: Set a timer and get him to start beading to create a necklace within the time limit.

✴ Dexterity test: Count all the pom-poms and then match them with the colour of the circle.

✴ Intelligence test: Take the alphabet blocks and spell his full name and age. Your child can also use a lightbox here and write the name of the superhero whose costume he is wearing.

THE POWER OF MAKE-BELIEVE

✷ Motor skill test: Make a superhero logo at the play dough station or draw it using paints or crayons.

✷ Responsiveness test: Build any superhero house on a Lego baseplate and explain it within three minutes.

✷ Numbers test: Play hopscotch (jumping while saying each number) to ensure he knows his numbers.

✷ Power test: Jump over all the blocks and create a large tile tower at the end of the obstacle course.

✷ Strength test: He needs to do whatever activity you have planned. If you have a basketball hoop at home, you can challenge him to score three baskets in a row. If you have roller skates at home, he can do three skating rounds without falling; bowling strikes; darts—pretty much anything that will challenge your child physically.

✷ Be lenient on the timer. If the timer is up, and they need a few more seconds or minutes, let them have it, just as long as they are enjoying the activity and are engaged.

✷ Once he has passed all the tests (and please make sure he passes all the tests), he can be awarded the certificate or a medal. Your child will actually feel like the greatest superhero at the end of this.

#KeySkills

☞ Role-play skills
☞ Language development skills
☞ Motor skills
☞ Cognitive development skills
☞ Creative skill enhancement

8. TIME MACHINE

As a child, didn't you love the *Faraway Tree* series by Enid Blyton where the children find a new land each time they go to the top of the magic tree? To mimic that, we can do a time machine at home through which your child can go to different countries, planets and time zones by merely stepping into a box!

#WhatYouNeed

- ☞ A large cardboard box into which your child can fit
- ☞ Paints or crayons and colour pens
- ☞ Chart paper
- ☞ Scissors, glue and tape
- ☞ A toilet paper roll

#HowtoPrep

- ✳ Open a large cardboard box and use the front part as a door. Paint the leftover toilet paper roll and glue it to the door from inside. Use it as the handle to open and close the door. Cut open a small rectangular slot from the back of the box for some ventilation.
- ✳ Put a sign outside that says 'TIME MACHINE'.
- ✳ Beneath that, paste a list of countries or cities that your child has read about or has visited.
- ✳ Below that, stick a paper plate, which can act as the steering wheel. Along the sides, put in the years starting from the year your child was born till fifty years later.

* Also, to hone his understanding of the alphabet, also paste below the steering small, coloured pieces of paper with each letter of the alphabet on them. This will be an alphabet keypad.
* Paste a number pad with numbers from 0–9.

#HowtoPlay

* For this activity, it is important to read up on different countries, monuments of the world, world cuisines, etc.
* Also, have a conversation with your child about time periods. Tell him how life was different when you were a child as compared to when his grandparents were children. It is also wise to introduce them to some science fiction books meant for children in which they can be exposed to the different imaginative ways one can envision the future.
* Once they have fully grasped the concept of time, both past and future, they can play with the Time Machine.
* To play, your child has to decide upon a country from the list and punch it into the alphabet keypad. Once he does that, he can go in and sit inside the machine and travel there. He can then tell you what he sees—monuments, animals, currency, flag, people, their clothes, their mannerisms, food, famous people of the time, etc. Listen to his stories. Give him prompts by asking if he saw a specific thing characteristic to that country or city.
* To travel to a different time zone, he has to punch the year into the numerical keypad, enter the machine and close the door. Ask him what he sees and you may be surprised—they

may see aliens, flying machines, flying animals, automated dinosaurs, robots operating planes, etc.

✷ Use this activity to increase your child's general knowledge about the world, while practising spelling and numbers through the keypads.

#KeySkills

☞ Creativity and imagination skills
☞ Cognitive reasoning skills
☞ Logical and practical application of knowledge

9. BE AN AUTHOR

Which child does not want to have his own book with his own name on the cover? That is such a treat and easily achievable.

#WhatYouNeed

☞ A hardbound book or a spiral notebook with blank pages
☞ A ruler
☞ Pencils, erasers, crayons

#HowtoPrep

✷ Draw a sequence of events telling a story involving a few human or animal characters in different places and settings that are relatable to a child, such as a grocery store, a garden, a beach, a mall, a coffee shop, a playground, a school. You can also print out various stories depicted in visual form and stick in the book. This is a time-consuming activity and takes some parental effort to ensure it follows a meaningful sequence.

* Leave space for five ruled lines at the bottom of each page.
* Ensure that each page has a prompt or a cue, which is highlighted in a different and bright colour. For example, if in the scene, a child drops her toy without noticing it—the clue can be the toy that was dropped. Your child can write a story based on that specific event in the scene.
* Always have a happy and satisfactory resolution in the climax. If a girl loses something in the story, it is found. If someone is robbed, the robber is caught. If there is danger, a superhero comes to save the day.
* Allow your child to illustrate the cover of the book and write their name on it as the author.
* When your child is done putting this entire book together, laminate and save this book as your child's very first!

#HowtoPlay

* Ask your child to look through the images you have thoughtfully and selectively curated for him in the form of a story.
* Ask him to make up a story based on the images. Prompt him along the way by asking him to look for the clues and then help him build the story to the climax.
* Assist him to write a few lines describing the story under each page in the space provided.

* Then finally to drawing the main characters or a scenario on the cover and putting his name there.
* Now show off the book to everyone and ask your child to read it aloud to all the family members and friends.

#KeySkills

- Language development
- Oral fluency
- Social and emotional development
- Vocabulary
- Sequencing and sorting skills
- Logical reasoning skills
- Reading, comprehension, writing skills
- Entrepreneurial skills

10. CARTON CITY

Ever imagined what it would be like to have a bird's eye view of the city we live in? This activity is perfect for the curious child and serves as a great activity to put it all in perspective.

#WhatYouNeed

- Empty milk and juice cartons
- Empty cans

- ☞ Paper bags
- ☞ Paints, colour pencils, crayons
- ☞ Chart paper, paper, cutter, glue and a broad tape

#HowtoPrep

- ✷ Use tape to create a road on a chart paper.
- ✷ Then take your milk and juice cartons and convert them into buildings. Cover them with white paper and paint the buildings in bright colours.
- ✷ Make some windows on a separate sheet, colour them, and cut and stick them onto the cartons so they look like houses. You can also use a cutter to cut open a door in each carton.
- ✷ Use paper to cover cans and draw in windows and doors on those as well.
- ✷ You can draw on brown paper bags and staple the top together to form a house. Draw doors, windows and even some graffiti.
- ✷ You can create a whole city by making one carton a hospital (with a red cross), another into a police station (with a cop drawing on the top), a library (with books drawn on it) and so on.
- ✷ Next, you can spread your child's miniature figurines around the city and place your toy cars on the roads.

#HowtoPlay

- ✷ Once your carton city is ready, let your child's imagination run wild. Let him tell you or other children all kinds of stories using this pretend play carton city.

#KeySkills

- 🤟 Creative thinking and imagination skills
- 🤟 Sensory motor skills
- 🤟 Gross motor skills
- 🤟 Cognitive, reasoning and application skills
- 🤟 Oral fluency

11. SUPERHERO HEADQUARTERS

If your child has a room full of superheroes, being the Superhero Boss would surely be his dream job! So, let us get his overactive imagination take flight doing what he loves most!

#WhatYouNeed

- 🤟 Sheets of paper, pen, paints, crayons, coloured paper
- 🤟 Play phones, play laptops, calculators, walkie-talkie sets
- 🤟 A pin board and Post-it notes

#HowtoPrep

- ✴ In this activity, you are the assistant and your child is the Superhero Boss—much like Nick Fury in the Avengers.
- ✴ Create a great superhero ambience in the room—use posters, figurines and other superhero paraphernalia as props to decorate.

* Set up a table with chairs as the Superhero Station. Trace your child's hand on a black chart paper and colour it in. This will form the hand scanner, which you can paste on the table.

* Cut small squares of paper to resemble keys on a computer keyboard and write various numbers and alphabets on them in the same way. Paste this near the hand scanner. You can also draw an eye and create an eye scanner.

* Set up some phones, calculators, real or toy laptops (anything with buttons really!) and a walkie-talkie set (if you have one) to make the place look like it's a control centre.

* Next, create a vision board of superheroes. Draw and colour in each of the superheroes. Label the drawings by writing their names below them along with a sentence of information (their specific superpower, their planet of origin, etc.) about each one of them.

* Now, this next part is the fun part. Ask your child about the kind of difficult situations superheroes have saved people from. Write down such situations on separate notecards and put them in a box. For example, a girl has been kidnapped and the villain is hiding her under a bridge.

* Set up the box of problem cards on the Superhero Station.

#HowtoPlay

* Let your child get comfortable with the Superhero Station—he may pretend to take calls and talk to the superheroes on the phone or through the walkie-talkie,

113

scan his fingerprints to gain access to the database of superheroes, etc.

✱ Next, he must remove one problem from the problem box. You, as his assistant, can also deliver the notecards to him one at a time and tell him a new situation has developed that requires his immediate attention. Let your child read the notecard and then assign it to a superhero on the vision board using Post-its. Then watch your child call the superhero on the phone (or through any other means of communication) and explain to him how he must solve the problem. He will need to walk the superhero through it; explain things step by step. He may get into a disagreement on the call, get excited, scream and shout through the call and then finally emerge victorious.

✱ Like this, you can keep coming up with various situations to allow your child to exercise his problem-solving skills and develop an extensive vocabulary while talking to his band of superheroes.

#KeySkills

☞ Logical reasoning skills
☞ Creative thinking and imagination skills
☞ Leadership skills
☞ Vocabulary
☞ Problem-solving skills

12. APPLE PICKING ORCHARD

Every child knows the famous adage, 'An apple a day keeps the doctor away', but do they know that there are over eleven types of apples? Time to learn some apple picking, sorting, cutting, juicing, saucing and much more through this activity.

#WhatYouNeed

- ꜱ Chart paper
- ꜱ Pens, art paints, crayons, brushes, glue and tape
- ꜱ Velcro dot patches
- ꜱ Baskets and organizers
- ꜱ Cash register or calculator
- ꜱ Cash box
- ꜱ Different varieties of apples
- ꜱ Plastic balls
- ꜱ Juice bottles
- ꜱ Buckets and pots

#HowtoPrep

✱ Cut out shapes of some tree trunks from chart paper and get your child to paint them brown, and then make the top of the trees and ask him to paint or colour them green. Once dried, put the trees together and stick them to a door or a wall.

✱ Use some plastic balls or crumbled pieces of paper and paint them red to resemble apples.

✱ Stick a velcro dot to each ball using a potent glue. Fix the other piece of the velcro dot on the tree and attach all the balls to the trees in this manner; they are guaranteed to stay on for a while.

✴ Now for the rest of the set-up. You can create an apple farm by setting up an organizer or a table with different kinds of apples in buckets or pots marking them with MRP stickers.

✴ Read up on and then explain to your child the various types of apples and their uses. It would be great if you could get samples of the red apple, the green apple, the golden delicious apple, the gala apple, etc. for your child to sample and determine how each tastes, so that they have adequate knowledge on apples, which they can regurgitate to their customers.

✴ Keep handy your cash register or calculator, some baskets and a cash box, to sell your apples.

✴ The next step is to make apple juice. Simple and easy—run the apples through a mixer, and just bottle the juice up.

✴ If you want to be adventurous, you can make apple sauce and put it in an airtight container and paste the MRP sticker on it. And finally, if you want to up the ante further, you can also create an apple crumble pie.

✴ Print a menu card with all the food on offer and put it on the table.

✴ If you have the time and the supplies, you can also do a farm set-up with some grass and leaves. You can also set up a seed table with various kinds of seeds and flower bulbs in pots, which can be sold to family and friends to make it more exciting for your child.

✳ Use number and colour sorting in this activity wherever
you can.

#HowtoPlay

✳ Be a customer at your child's beautiful apple orchard.

✳ When you and your family members enter the orchard,
your child must give you a basket. You can keep the apples
you pick from the orchard (the plastic balls from the 'trees')
in here. Give the basket full of apples back to your child
who will then count and put all the balls into a huge pot
(a pretend mixer) and then serve you with your choice of
apple juice or apple sauce.

✳ Finally, you may also buy some real apples from the ones
displayed in the buckets and even add on a slice of the
apple pie.

✳ Do not forget to praise the apple orchard and pay for
your purchases.

#KeySkills

☞ Cognitive skills
☞ Logical reasoning skills
☞ Sensory motor skills
☞ Creative thinking skills

13. PICNIC

Nothing is as exciting as a beautiful picnic set-up that your child
has put together.

#WhatYouNeed

- All your pretend vegetables, fruits, breads, butter, etc.
- Real fruits
- Bread and cheese
- Juices
- A basket or a box
- Candy (optional)
- Picnic mat (or any mat or sheet)
- Sunglasses, hat and umbrella (optional)
- Battery-operated candles (optional)
- Tablemats, paper plates, spoons, forks, glasses, paper napkins (use disposable, if your child is under the age of three)
- Stuffed toys
- Flowers

#HowtoPlay

★ Tell your child that today is Picnic Day, so he must pack all the essential items and clear an area in the house, perhaps on the terrace or the garden where the picnic can take place.

★ Ask them what they would like to eat at the picnic. If they say sandwiches or cookies—involve your child in making them.

★ Ask your child to take out the picnic basket or a small carry-on box and pack the picnic mat and all the other essentials in the basket. Ask him to do all the packing himself and to check that everything is there.

* Tell him it will be sunny so he must carry his sunglasses and a hat, and maybe an umbrella for some shade.

* Once you get to the picnic spot, ask your child to spread out the mat, place the table mats and tableware on it. Place the artificial food in the bowls and the real food in the plates and pour the juice into everyone's glass. Tell him to decorate the picnic space with the flowers. And finally, to wear his sunglasses/hat and set up his umbrella.

* Your picnic is now ready and everyone can sit back and enjoy. If the family members are busy to join him in the pretend picnic, help him set up the picnic with his stuffed animals or superhero characters. If a little mess is made, it is fine! Best memories are sometimes made messy!

#KeySkills

☞ Fine motor skills
☞ Analytical skills
☞ Collaboration skills

14. AIRPLANE RIDE

It is time to fly away! Children love airports and airplanes and the idea of flying away to a new place! Let your child pretend play to be a pilot and fly his own plane and take you places!

#WhatYouNeed

- ☞ Paper and pens
- ☞ Six to seven chairs
- ☞ Table
- ☞ Gadgets around the house like remote controls, phones, I-pads, walkie-talkies, etc.,
- ☞ Cash register
- ☞ Binoculars
- ☞ Pilot costume or simply a white cap
- ☞ Scissors, glue and tape

#HowtoPrep

✱ Put your child in a white shirt, a tie and a pair of black pants. Make an identity card with some crayons or pens. The ID should have his name on it and also his photograph to make it look more real. If you have a white cap, let him put that on as well and you have a pilot in the house.

✱ Design your tickets and boarding passes. Tell your child to write the name of the airport on them and other details like the terminal, the flight number, the seat numbers, etc. He can draw and decorate these in any way he wants. Make some more chits with the seat numbers to stick on the pretend airplane chairs.

✱ Make a ticket counter. Store all the unsold tickets on a counter in a basket, with rubber stamps, if you have any.

✱ Arrange a table with all kinds of gadgets in your house so it may function as a cockpit; place a chair there too. Behind that, place a bunch of chairs in rows, like in an airplane.

Stick the seat numbers behind the chairs. If you have eye masks and bedsheets, you may place them on every seat. In case you have sashes lying around, they can function as seat belts!

✴ If some seats are going empty, you can place your child's stuffed toys and animals on the seats and buckle them in.

✴ Keep a tray or a bar cart or a trolley of snacks handy— popcorn, chips, peanuts, cereal bars, granola bars, some bottles of water and other things can be placed on it.

✴ You can even put fairy lights or night lights for night mode. Your passengers can take a nap during this time.

#HowtoPlay

✴ Let all the passengers line up at the ticket counter where the pilot himself will stamp your tickets, give you your boarding pass and ticket and walk you into the airplane.

✴ He will instruct you that you are to remain seated at all times and wear your seatbelts and only when the pilot announces it's safe, can you get up.

✴ He will check the seat number on your ticket and match it with the seat numbers at the back of the chairs, ushering you to the correct one.

✴ Settle yourself in your seat and put on your seatbelt. Then put your carry-on luggage under your chair. If you have a blanket or an eye mask on your seat, you may use it and pretend to be asleep when it is time to sleep.

✴ The pilot can take his seat in the cockpit and periodically make announcements about the weather, the turbulence, the snack cart that will shortly be around, and other important things about safety.

✳ Your child can then don the role of the steward or stewardess and serve the snacks. He can go to each seat and ask the passengers if they some want some water or a snack, show them options and then provide them with what they need.

✳ Finally, your child can go back to being the pilot. He can return to the cockpit and press all the gadgets on the table to manoeuvre the plane and then finally land it. Everyone should act delighted and congratulate him on a successful flight and a smooth journey.

✳ Keep conversing with the pilot during the flight as a passenger—request to see the cockpit, ask him plenty of questions about the plane, the control station, the cockpit, the gadgets he uses, how he lands the plane, etc. Even if he does not have all the answers, watch your child make up creative responses.

#KeySkills

☞ Vocabulary
☞ Sensory motor skills
☞ Logical thinking skills
☞ Leadership
☞ Critical and creative thinking skills

15. BIRTHDAY PARTY FOR A DOLL OR SUPERHERO

If you want your child to realize how much effort it really takes to put on a party for him, make him plan one for his stuffed animal, or favourite superhero or doll! This activity is designed to keep your child busy for a few hours. So do this one on a day when you need a break!

#WhatYouNeed

- ⊱ Tables
- ⊱ Toy organizers
- ⊱ Play dough
- ⊱ Art and craft materials
- ⊱ Toys of all kinds
- ⊱ Disposable plates and cutlery
- ⊱ Party decorations
- ⊱ Birthday card

#HowtoPrep

- ✱ First discuss with your child and select a theme around which to plan the party.
- ✱ Then simply spread everything you've planned for the party out on different tables as shown below:
  - ✱ Lots of art and craft materials including party hats, streamers, balloons, paper, paints and crayons.
  - ✱ Plain notecards on which you can write birthday wishes or birthday cards.

* On another table or organizer, place toys, cars, dolls or books or anything your child has in bigger numbers that can be packaged.

* On the next table, keep play dough in different colours to make the play dough cake; you can use real candles.

* Use buntings and some string or ribbon for decoration. You may also ask your child to paint, draw or practice some fingerprint painting on the buntings.

* Keep party plates, cups, napkins, forks and spoons on another table.

* Arrange pretend food, fruits and vegetables. You can include some real items that are spill-proof such as bread, jam and some candy bars or lollipops.

* If you want to make an easy twenty-minute cake, take all the baking supplies out: measuring cups, a weighing scale, a butter knife, a mixer, some milk, some Oreo biscuits, a chocolate bar and some baking powder. This one will need supervision at the time of baking. Empty two packets of Oreo biscuits into a bowl and grind them. Pour in half a cup of milk and then add a teaspoon of baking powder. Bake for ten to fifteen minutes and voila! You have an Oreo cake. Coat it with Nutella or a melted chocolate bar and top it with some vanilla ice cream if you want.

#HowtoPlay

* If your child has a favourite doll, toy or stuffed animal, give that toy a birth date and ask your child if he wants to put together a birthday party for him/her?

* Explain to your child what each station contains and what is required of him to make the birthday party a big success. Tell him he needs to decorate the room for the big birthday party, put together the presents, bag them, tag them, paint and colour the invitation cards, lay the plates and cups and cake in the middle of the table, lay out the pretend food and decorate the room and the table as he deems fit.

* Depending on your child's age, you can help out with some of the work like filling out the invitation cards or putting up the buntings.

* Now, leave the room and allow your child to creatively put this together. Allow him to use the supplies laid out on the table to execute the birthday party as he pleases and to the best of his ability.

* Do not forget to compliment the pretty mess of a birthday party that he creates!

#KeySkills

- Creativity and imagination skills
- Logical thinking skills
- Organization and execution skills
- Sensory motor skills
- Problem-solving skills

CHAPTER 6

#MakeBelieveMagic

*A child's play is not simply a reproduction of what
he has experienced, but a creative reworking of
the impressions he has acquired.*

—LEV VYGOTSKY

Most of the activities listed hereunder are based on certain professions. They require a greater exercise of imagination not just in conceptualizing the activities but in their execution as well. The activities create a pretend play zone where creative use of language and inventiveness make the activities more enjoyable. Ensure that your child relates tales of adventures to you while pretend playing in his new avatars. These can be undertaken by children in the age group of three to six years and some can also be taken up by two-year-olds who show an inclination towards pretend play with adult supervision.

1. ZOOKEEPER

Owning a zoo is as much fun as visiting one—perhaps more! You get to designate spaces for different animals, feed and bathe them and do a lot of fun things! So, let us pretend to be zookeepers!

#WhatYouNeed

 - A bunch of toy animals (stuffed animals, wooden animals, miniature animals, etc.)
 - Cardboard boxes
 - Wires or pipe cleaners
 - Paper and crayons
 - Bowls
 - A large bucket

#HowtoPrep

 * Open all your boxes and place wires or pipe cleaners as bars at their openings.
 * Draw the various food items for each kind of animal in the zoo, such as meat, grass, insects, worms, etc. and let your child cut them out with a pair of child friendly scissors.

#HowtoPlay

 * First read up on animals and their chief characteristics, what they eat, fun facts about them, and discuss them with your child so he understands more about animals.
 * Now, he can place all the animals in the boxes with bars that you created which will serve as enclosures.

* Designate a feeding time and put the cut-outs of food into some bowls and let your child keep the bowls in the appropriate cages.

* Designate a time for the animal baths. When your child bathes, he can take the animals in a bucket into the bathroom and wash all of them.

* This is a fun activity and can keep your child engaged for a week or longer as he cares for the animals in the zoo.

#KeySkills

☞ Creative and imagination skills
☞ Social and emotional skills
☞ Leadership

2. BANKER

Have you ever taken your child to the bank and watched his befuddled face as you attempted to teach him how to cash a cheque? Or has he ever asked a lot of questions about banks and bankers: What do they do? Why do we keep going to the bank? This activity will help satiate his curiosity and confusion about the banking system and expand his worldview and vocabulary.

#WhatYouNeed

- 🖙 Formalwear for your child
- 🖙 Printout of a cheque or a cancelled cheque
- 🖙 Computer or a calculator
- 🖙 Play phone and play laptop
- 🖙 Two shoeboxes
- 🖙 Play money and coins
- 🖙 Paper and pens
- 🖙 Play passport

#HowtoPrep

- ✸ Set up your child's table as the bank teller's desk; use a calculator, a laptop, a phone, lots of play money and coins in a box and some papers, pens, clipboards and printouts of cheques.
- ✸ Keep the check-in form simple with details as follows— Name, Age, Savings or Checking Account, Credit Card or Debit Card and Telephone Number.
- ✸ Cover the two shoeboxes with black chart paper or paint them. Write 'SAFE DEPOSIT BOX' on both.
- ✸ Get your child in his professional banker ensemble.

#HowtoPlay

- ✸ Ask your child to man his bank teller's desk. You can go as a customer who needs to deposit some money.
- ✸ When you get to his counter, you can request to open an account for a safe deposit box.

✳ He will ask you for your identity card and check your name and photograph, after which he will write your name and age on the check-in form, and give you a cheque on which you will fill in the amount of money you are depositing.

✳ He will go through the form with you and check-mark as applicable.

✳ He will take the cheque and deposit it into your account by placing it in the shoebox safe deposit box and handing the box to you. If you have letter stickers, you can put them on the safe deposit box to spell out your name.

✳ You may keep your wallet, passport and other items of importance inside the box, hand it back to him and ask him to look after it.

✳ He will then give you a handwritten receipt to show the amount you have deposited in the bank and hand a credit card for you to use.

✳ If your child is older and has an advance understanding of mathematical concepts, you can also ask him to do a basic interest calculation.

#KeySkills

↬ Cognitive and reasoning skills
↬ Problem-solving skills
↬ Comprehension skills
↬ Vocabulary
↬ Numerical skills

3. PHOTOGRAPHER

Children love to take pictures! Teaching them how it is also a career path can make them understand the art and skill behind taking a good picture.

#WhatYouNeed

- Few sheets of coloured paper
- Digital camera (an iPad could work if you do not have this)
- Chart paper, scissors, paints
- A frame from which one can hang a cloth sheet
- Pens
- Some decorative props from around the house to create a backdrop
- A blank journal

#HowtoPrep

* First, read up on photographers and photography to your child. Explain the concept of landscape, portrait, lifestyle and product photography. Product photography is for people who want to showcase their products commercially; others who want to show people what using their product would be like, resort to lifestyle photography. When people want to commemorate events such as birthdays, anniversaries or weddings, and want aesthetic images of such occasions to save for posterity, a photographer saves the day.

✳ Show him a few good pictures and a few bad ones and explain the differences between the two. Once your child has grasped the basics of photography, hand him an iPad or a digital camera and explain the basic buttons and features such as how to zoom in and out, etc.

✳ Give your child's photography studio a name and put it on the door, for example, 'Aiden's Photo Studio'. Little details like this can get your child in the mood and mindset of the character he is about to play.

✳ Your child can also draw a couple of cameras on chart paper, cut them out, paint them and then stick them around the walls to give the room the look of a photography studio.

✳ Decorate your child's set aesthetically—you can hang sheets in various colours from a frame, curtain rods or a door. Put up some fairy lights or electric candles. In the absence of colourful sheets, you can hang streamers, scarves—anything that could serve as a good backdrop.

✳ Keep props handy, such as stuffed animals, unicorns, cute pillows, terrariums, crates, photo frames, lights, lamps, etc.

✳ Keep a stack of forms in the studio where each customer can circle the services they want. If they want a photoshoot with or without props, how many shots do they need and so on.

#HowtoPlay

✳ Once the scene is set, he can invite friends and family into his studio for a photography session. He will ask them one by one to fill the form. They can select the services they want and take their place in front of the hanging sheets and start off.

✸ When you are posing for the camera, ask your child to zoom in on your prop or your face. Ensure you ask him to keep showing you the images and that you commend him on the photos. But if you feel he needs a bit of help with the images, you can gracefully and gently offer suggestions like how to adjust and handle the settings on the camera and get the right focus.

✸ Your child can also use his stuffed animals or a pet or even his superhero figures and continue his own photoshoots. Watch him try to get it right from different angles and mix up the props and play with concepts to create magical pictures.

✸ To encourage him further, print out some of the images and give them to him to archive in his photography journal.

#KeySkills

☞ Creative thinking and imagination
☞ Logical reasoning skills
☞ Cognitive skills
☞ Social and emotional skills

4. OPHTHALMOLOGIST AKA YOUR EYE SPECIALIST

This activity may not be as great a way to check your eyes as it is to test your child's knowledge of the alphabet!

#WhatYouNeed

- A few pairs of numberless eye glasses with transparent lenses
- A few pairs of eye glasses in small boxes from around the house
- Two leftover toilet paper cardboard rolls or a pair of binoculars
- Sheets of paper
- Eye drops
- Lens solution
- Flashlight
- Book
- Clipboard

#HowtoPrep

- Read up on eye doctors and how they test eyes. Describe to your child what your last eye check-up felt like. Talk about nearsightedness and far-sightedness. Once he has grasped the concept, he is going to be excited to explore it as the doctor!
- Get your child into character. Set up the room like an ophthalmologist's clinic. Get him to wear a long white

shirt or jacket so it looks like a doctor's coat. You can even make him wear an identity card around his neck.

* Next, take a print of the eye test chart or make this yourself by putting the letters in a pyramid form (from big to small) and stick it onto a whiteboard, blackboard or on a wall.

* Then keep all the glasses and doctor's paraphernalia ready on a table.

* Keep a clipboard ready with the patient information forms.

* Keep two chairs in the waiting area at the entrance.

#HowtoPlay

* When a patient (you or any other family member) visits for an eye check-up, your child, as the receptionist, can first ask them to take a seat in the waiting area and then ask them to fill in the patient form with all their information like their name, phone number and their eyesight number, if any.

* He then checks the form and asks them to sit a little further away from the letters of the eye test chart on the wall so they can try to read the chart. The doctor will tell them if they are right or wrong.

* Once that is done, the child as the doctor analyses how much the patient's eyesight number has increased or decreased and asks them to try on different lenses and read the chart again.

* Next, the doctor will ask the patient to use the toilet rolls or the binoculars and look through them to read out loud from a book.

* Finally, he will tell the patient if they need to take some medicines or eye drops, hand those to them with a new pair of glasses from which you can magically see everything clearly.
* The patient must thank the doctor profusely and can now leave the clinic with better eyesight!

#KeySkills

- Creativity and imagination skills
- Visual processing skills
- Social and emotional skills
- Logical reasoning skills

5. DENTIST

Going to a dentist can be intimidating for kids and adults alike. But being the dentist for a bit can evoke empathy and understanding for the profession and lessen their fear. For this activity, use the exact same set-up as the ophthalmologist's clinic, but just with different set of tools.

#WhatYouNeed

- Two chairs and a table for the waiting room; some magazines or books
- Toothbrushes of different kinds and sizes; dental floss

- Different kinds of toothpastes
- Flashlight
- Soap
- Strips of white chewing gum
- Clipboard with patient information forms and a pen
- Medicine box with different kinds of child or adult medication

#HowtoPrep

* First, discuss with your child what happens if you do not look after your teeth—there can be gum decay, fractured teeth and cavities that require fillings, a root canal or worse, an extraction. If your child has milk teeth, it is time to tell them their teeth will fall off but will grow back once the tooth fairy comes in and takes the fallen tooth away leaving behind some money or a present in exchange for it.

* Read up on the daily practices of looking after one's teeth. Tell your child about your first visit to the dentist and what it was like. It is helpful to show them the structure and composition of the mouth through images or diagrams. Take your child to the dentist if he has not already been there.

* Once your child has grasped these concepts, and if he would like to be a dentist, get to the preparations—first do your clinic set-up the same way you did for the ophthalmologist.

* Keep your calculator, cash register and cash box ready along with your medicine box.

✳ Set up all the brushes, toothpastes, floss packs on the table along with some wipes and tissues.

✳ Next, make your dental impression. Take a bar of soap and melt it ever so slightly in a microwave. Once it is a bit gooey, press in your white square chewing gum pieces in it to resemble a real dental impression.

#HowtoPlay

✳ When the patients (family members, friends, stuffed animals, toys) come in, your child should make them wait in the waiting room and have them fill in the patient form with all their details including the problem they are facing (tooth decay, gum inflammation, cavity, pain, yellowing teeth, etc.).

✳ Next, he must use his medical equipment to examine the issue using a flashlight. He can give an injection or prescribe medication if need be.

✳ Once he is done with this, he can give instructions for dental care. He can use the soap impression piece to show the patient how they must brush and floss their teeth correctly.

✳ He can prescribe different kinds of toothbrushes and toothpastes as well.

#KeySkills

☞ Creative thinking and imagination skills
☞ Logical reasoning skills
☞ Sensory motor skills
☞ Verbal expression skills
☞ Role-play skills

6. DOCTOR-DOCTOR

Remember playing Doctor-Doctor with your friends or cousins and operating upon your parents when you were young? The game is not just fun but can also prepare your child for a doctor's visit that he may find fearful. Playing Doctor-Doctor will help him conquer the fear of the unknown.

#WhatYouNeed

- ➤ A tray or a bag with all your doctor supplies ranging from a stethoscope, a thermometer, an injection, a box of band-aid, some creams, nasal spray, eye drops, a flashlight, latex gloves, syringes, droppers, earbuds, cotton, tissues, measuring cups, gauze bandage, and a whole bunch of medicines
- ➤ Table and chair
- ➤ Doctor's briefcase
- ➤ Clipboard
- ➤ An array of dolls and figurines as patients

#HowtoPrep

- ✳ Take a printout of a diagram of the human body with its various parts. Set up an area where the patients can be examined: a table or a bed. Place a folded bedsheet and a small pillow for comfort. Keep all the doctor's supplies close at hand in a tray or in the open briefcase.
- ✳ Ask your child to wear a loose white shirt, hang a stethoscope around his neck and put on a pair of glasses.

✳ You can also make him an identity card with his picture and name on it, as we did for other activities.

✳ As he takes up each doll or figurine or other patients, he can circle that part in the diagram of the human body where the patient has pain. Then he may check their eyes, nose, throat, temperature, blood pressure and heartbeat. He may put in pretend eye drops. He may also give an injection if necessary. If there is a wound, he should put a Band-Aid or gauze bandage, and finally prescribe medicines.

✳ Let your child first play Doctor-Doctor with his dolls and toys. Once he is used to behaving like a doctor and has become used to the system, family members can join in and go to their child with a pretend ailment.

#KeySkills

☞ Social and emotional skills
☞ Practical application skills
☞ Cognitive and reasoning skills
☞ Logical thinking skills
☞ Interpersonal skills

7. LIBRARIAN

Libraries are the most magical places. Set up a library in any cozy corner in your home and get your child obsessed with the magic of the written word.

#WhatYouNeed

- Books arranged on shelves or in a cupboard or on a table
- Two chart papers
- Two white papers
- Pencils or pens
- Marker
- String (optional)
- Passport-size photograph of your child
- A thermometer
- Play cash register
- A beanbag or a layered mattress or cushions to make a comfortable reading nook.

#HowtoPrep

* Cut out a chart paper in the shape of a credit card. Put a passport-size photograph of your child on the top right corner and make a library card in your child's name, for example, 'Aidan's Library Card'. At the back of the card, draw some lines and write 'Name of Book' and 'Date of Issue'.

* Put up a sign that says 'Reading Hours' near the books and put down the time slot during which you want your child to read.

* You can also make a sign that says 'Library is Open' on one side and 'Library is Closed' on the other side. Punch two holes in it and hang it anywhere near the pretend library's entrance.

* You can also put up a 'List of Books Checked Out' with space below the heading to write the book names.

#HowtoPlay

* This is an ongoing practice and not a one-time play. Reading hour should be a permanent part of your child's routine, so whenever you want your child to read, flip the sign to 'Library is Open' and create a little reading nook that is comfortable and attractive. It could have a beanbag, a small reading table, a rocking chair or any space your child does not use on a daily basis.

* During that hour, your child can select as many books as he wants. He should write the name of the book at the back of the library card along with the date. If he is having trouble writing, you may help him out.

* If parents are playing the role of the librarian, they must scan the book (scanner can be a thermometer or a play cashier machine. Enter the details in the 'List of Books Checked Out'. Stick a Post-it note that says 'Checked Out' on the book and then hand it over to the child.

* Your child can then sit in the reading corner and read. Once the book is read, the child must return it to the librarian to avoid a late penalty.

* You can also make a bookmark that your child can use. Cut a 10 x 2-inch paper rectangle and write your child's name on it (for example, 'Kiaan's Bookmark') and you can write a literary quote or draw on it as well to make it interesting. Punch a hole on top and put a string through it. Explain

to your child that a bookmark is used to remember the page you left off at. These can be a permanent fixture in the reading nook along with the books.

✳ If your child does not return the book after the reading hour, he gets a penalty and the parents can decide what it would be (no TV time, no favourite meal or snack, etc.) so that he learns to take his books back on time.

✳ Let your child also play the librarian and allow him to check your books out. Discuss the job of a librarian with him in detail so he can role-play with siblings and friends too.

#KeySkills

☞ Reading and comprehension skills
☞ Communication skills
☞ Vocabulary and language development skills
☞ Visual-processing skills
☞ Logic and reasoning skills

8. DIY STAYCATION

If you really wanted to go on a trip but it did not work out, you are probably thinking there can be no fun ways in which you can make a weekend in your own home fun and exciting for your child. A DIY staycation is here to tell you, you can!

#WhatYouNeed

- ☞ Some trays or a trolley table
- ☞ Ingredients to make your favourite brunch
- ☞ Crayons
- ☞ Cardboard sheets
- ☞ Flowers, candles, fragrant oils
- ☞ Bathrobes and matching sleepwear

#HowtoPrep

- ✸ Get a lavish spread prepared for brunch—you can make eggs, toast, orange juice, coffee, tea, scones, cupcakes, doughnuts, chocolates, cookies, croissants, pancakes, the works! Order some of it in so you do not have to make it all and actually feel like it is a vacation.

- ✸ Plate everything beautifully with flowers and candles on a trolley table or just use a few trays.

- ✸ Keep your bathrobes ready. Make up your bed with a fresh new comforter and put on some fragrant oils on an oil burner or burn a scented candle to get the feeling of being in a hotel room.

- ✸ Make a 'Do Not Disturb' sign and hang it on the knob of your bedroom door.

#HowtoPlay

- ✸ Ask your child if he would like to check into a hotel, order room service, eat in the bed with a bathrobe on and watch a good movie. Ask him if he would like to recreate that experience at home?

✱ If he says yes, select a good movie you can all enjoy as a family, put on those bathrobes, put the 'Do Not Disturb' sign on the door, send out your outfits to the laundry service, and bring in the trolley table on which you have set up the lavish brunch.

✱ Then turn off all your phones, ask others in the house not to disturb you, put on some face masks, paint your nails, drink your coffee or champagne, engage in a pillow fight with your child, watch the movie and enjoy your feast!

✱ Even if you are planning a movie night with your family at home, this is a fun way to make it more interesting.

#KeySkills

☞ Creativity and imagination skills
☞ Cognitive and reasoning skills
☞ Social and emotional skills

9. OFFICE WORKER

Adulting is not really all that fun, but when you were little, it was all you wanted to do—work like Mommy and Daddy in an office. But office environments can be quite intimidating for young impressionable minds. So why not recreate them in the safety of your home? Let them work too while you are at work or working from home!

#WhatYouNeed

- ☞ Office supplies such as paper clips, phones, computers (real or pretend), papers of all kinds, notebooks
- ☞ Kid-friendly scissors, tape, glue, art supplies, coloured Post-its, colour pens and pencils, some old books or diaries which you no longer use
- ☞ Suitcase or briefcase (toy or real)

#HowtoPrep

- ✸ Set up a workstation for your child in his room and set out the office supplies on his desk.
- ✸ Keep his formal 'office' clothes ready.

#HowtoPlay

- ✸ Tell your child it is now working hours, so he needs to go to work, just like you do. He needs to dress up, put in a few important things such as a play phone, laptop, etc. in his office bag and then get to office (his room) where the office set-up is and get to work.
- ✸ Now let him get busy answering calls, marking important meetings, discussing work, exploring all the office supplies, doing art and craft or merely making a mess attempting to use a baby stapler or anything else.
- ✸ If you have something important to do, set up an office for your children and you will not be disturbed for some time because they want to be 'busy' doing 'office work' as well.

#KeySkills

- Logical reasoning skills
- Cooperation, collaboration and organizational skills
- Motor skills
- Sequencing and sorting skills

10. I SPY

Every time things go missing around my house, I ask my in-house detective to locate them. While he has not always been successful at finding them, he has always had a great deal of fun trying!

#WhatYouNeed

- Flashlight
- Stamp pad and stamps
- Magnifying glass
- Large paintbrush or make-up brush
- Tape
- Envelopes
- Cardboard box
- Notebook and pen
- Earbuds
- Reusable Ziploc bags
- Lint remover (optional)
- Any toy that can operate as a scanner

#HowtoPrep

✳ For this activity, you will need to do all the preparation yourself.

✳ Take a cardboard box or your child's toy suitcase and use chart paper to write your child's name on it in this manner: 'Detective Kyle's Mystery-Solving Box'.

✳ Place the following things in Ziplog bags and label them accordingly:

* a magnifying glass neatly labelled 'Detective's Magnifying Glass'
* earbuds labelled 'Swabs'
* a notebook labelled 'Mystery Journal'
* a flashlight with a label
* a reel of Scotch tape labelled 'Fingerprint Tape'
* a paintbrush labelled 'Fingerprint Dusting Brush'
* a stamp pad labelled 'Fingerprinting Kit'

✳ Keep some empty Ziploc bags and label them 'Evidence'.

✳ Keep some envelopes in a box labelled 'Secret Clues'.

✳ If you have a scanner such as a card machine, a calculator or a cash register, you can use that to scan the scene and label it 'Scanner'. Alternatively, a lint roller can also be used for the same purpose.

✳ If you have access to an iPad or a camera that your child can use to take photographs of the 'scene', that can be put in the box as well.

#HowtoPlay

✳ Once your box is packaged and labelled, tell your child there is a mystery in the house to be solved—an item has gone missing and he needs to help you find it. For that, he needs to become a detective. Give him the box and tell him about the items in it.

✴ Let him explore the items and play with them—he can dust for fingerprints with the brush, test fingerprints with the tape and the stamp pad and then match them with the fingerprints of the suspects (family members) in your house, find clues and collect them in the Ziplog bags, use his magnifying glass and flashlight to inspect the corners of your house. He can use the earbuds to gather the evidence in the Ziploc bags.

✴ If he can write, he should journal his observations and the evidence he has collected.

✴ He can interrogate everyone in the house about where the item was last seen and take pictures of those locations as he goes about his search.

✴ Allow your child to lead this and enjoy the process of searching and taping and swabbing. Try and come up with missing items every few weeks for him to dig into his detective box. I intentionally hide items in places where my son may not easily look so he can enjoy the process of searching for the missing items longer.

#KeySkills

☞ Creativity and imagination skills
☞ Cognitive and reasoning skills
☞ Critical thinking skills
☞ Problem-solving skills

11. VET

Going to the doctor for yourself spells all kinds of anxiety, but taking your puppy or your dog is even worse. But if your child is the vet, it is a whole different situation.

#WhatYouNeed

- Paper, pens, water colours and crayons
- Doctor's supplies—stethoscope, play injections, Band-Aids, thermometer
- Clipboard
- Box or tray
- Medicines that are lying around the house
- Measuring tape and/or weighing scale

#HowtoPrep

- Dress your child in an oversized white shirt for dramatic effect (it can be borrowed from one of the parents).
- Use your child's room to set the clinic up. Keep a chair near his bed. The bed can be used to check the animal patients.
- Next to the chair will be the table with all the doctor's supplies well laid out. Keep the box of medicines on the table as well. You can paint a sign with your child's name on the door, for example, 'Dr Serena's Pet Clinic' with a red cross painted next to it.
- Place the clipboard with several sheets of papers and a pen to a write, on the table.

* Some distance away from the bed, you can create a waiting room (put a sign on the wall signifying that). Put two chairs in the waiting room and keep a small table with some animal magazines or books from your child's library on it for the people waiting.

* Get out all your stuffed animals, dolls, Peppa Pig characters, etc. and line them up in the waiting room.

#HowtoPlay

* If you have a pet at home, your pet can be the first patient.

* Your child can ask you to wait in the waiting room with your pet and read while you are there. He can also offer you water while you wait.

* Once you are taken into the doctor's clinic, he can ask you to put your pet on the bed where he will examine him using his instruments and even give an injection if necessary. He will also check his weight on a weighing scale and let you know if it's high or low.

* He will then write a prescription for your pet (on the sheets of paper on the clipboard) and ask you to visit the pharmacy to buy the medicines. You may thank the doctor at this point and leave as a happy pet-owner.

* At the pharmacy, your doctor magically becomes the pharmacist, takes the prescription, hands over the medicine to you and tells you how many times a day you need to give it to your pet.

* The entire array of stuffed animals in the house can now be seen by the doctor one by one.

✳ Once you have shown him how to set this play up, he will do it again and again by himself as and when he feels like playing vet.

#KeySkills

☞ Logical reasoning skills
☞ Vocabulary
☞ Social and emotional skills
☞ Planning, organization and execution skills

12. POLICEMAN

For this one, you have to be good at building a story! Tell your child something has gone missing in the house (a T-shirt, a ketchup bottle, etc.). Tell him you need him to be a policeman for the day and investigate the case of the missing item.

#WhatYouNeed

☞ **An old white or black blanket or cloth**
☞ **Fabric paints**
☞ **Bedsheet**
☞ **Two chairs**
☞ **Sunglasses**
☞ **String**
☞ **Cardboard, paper and some colour pens**

- Cap
- Two bangles or bracelets
- Safety pins
- Flashlight (optional)
- Binoculars (optional)
- Toy gun (optional)
- Walkie-Talkie or an old remote control or toy phone or any other similar gadget
- Whistle (optional)

#HowtoPrep

* Dress your child up like a cop.
* Make a vest from any old cloth you have—paint it using fabric paint and put the word 'POLICE' at the back and front. This does not require stitching, buttons or anything of the sort. Just cut through two holes for the arms and one for the head, and have your child wear it on top of his clothes.
* Next, we need a badge—a simple way to make this is to trace and cut out a star shape from a sheet of cardboard, write the words 'POLICE' on it and let your child colour it black, silver, gold, grey or red. String the badge and put it around his neck.
* You can also make an ID card with his passport-size picture and details.
* Put a toy gun under his belt.
* If he is a fan of flashlight or binoculars, let him carry those around, or even a pretend walkie-talkie.
* He needs a pair of sunglasses and a hat now—if you do not have a cap at home, cover any other hat you may have with

black chart paper. Make and attach the same star-shaped badge at the front of the hat.

✳ For handcuffs—two adult-size bangles strung together with a string is all you need.

✳ For the jail—take the largest bedsheet you can find and two stools or tall chairs. Spread the chairs apart and drape the bedsheet over them, so it looks like a rectangular tent. This can be the jail. You can draw jail bars on the bedsheet (if it is an old bedsheet) or just put up the signs 'POLICE STATION' and 'JAIL' at the spot.

#HowtoPlay

✳ So, now you tell your child about the lost item. He has to take up the case and solve it.

✳ You can ask him to retrace the footsteps of the person who used the item last.

✳ Egg him on by giving him clues. Urge him to search the entire house using his flashlight and binoculars, all the while calling out on his pretend walkie-talkie and blowing his whistle. Ensure that he speaks to everyone who lives in the house. Involve the entire family in the mystery that needs to be solved.

✳ Finally, pin it on Daddy who finished the lost item—the ketchup bottle—and hid the bottle so no one would know.

✳ The culprit has to be handcuffed at gunpoint and taken to jail. Daddy has to be read his rights. The culprit can also apologize and then be let out from the makeshift jail.

#KeySkills

- ☞ Emotional and social skills
- ☞ Cognitive skills
- ☞ Memory skills
- ☞ Logical reasoning skills
- ☞ Interpersonal skills

13. DINNER FOR TWO AT THE RESTAURANT

Involve your child in arranging a dinner date night with your partner!

#WhatYouNeed

- ☞ Chef's hat
- ☞ Apron
- ☞ Sheets of paper
- ☞ Pens
- ☞ Table setting items (table mats, plates, cutlery, condiments, flowers, a centrepiece)
- ☞ Electric candles (optional)

#HowtoPrep

- ✳ Tell your child to prep for the dinner—it could be arranged on your child's play table or a duvet on the floor with candles and floral set-ups or on the dining table.

Select the venue in your home together with your child and create an ambience—switch on some music, spread out some flowers, put up some candles or fairy lights, and lay out the table mats, plates, cutlery, etc. Involve your child in all the preparations and allow his suggestions to lead the setting.

* Print a menu with images of the food available and the name and prices of the dishes.

* Take a white sheet of paper and create a signboard, for example, 'Rishab's Restaurant'. If your child can write, then you can also ask him to do place cards.

* Keep another piece of paper ready with the bill.

* Dress your child in an apron and a chef's hat and ask him to be ready as your server.

* Keep the food ready in the kitchen to be served.

#HowtoPlay

* Once all set, Mom and Dad can get ready for date night.

* Your child can come to call you for dinner. Accompany him to his restaurant and tell him how beautiful it is.

* Once you are seated, he will offer you the menu. Ask him questions about his restaurant, the menu and the dishes he specializes in.

* Once you have ordered from the menu, he will bring you your dishes along with some water or a pre-prepared drink.

* Once date night is concluded, you can thank him for his service and tell him you will recommend his restaurant to many people.

✷ Ask for the bill and pay for what you ate. Tip generously.

✷ Remember to take a picture with the owner-cum-server.

#KeySkills

↣ Logical reasoning skills

↣ Social and emotional skills

↣ Reading and comprehending behaviours

↣ Practical application of theory

14. CAMPSITE HOLIDAY

Remember back when you were a child, when your parents said you all would be taking a holiday? What was the most fun part about it? The preparation, the planning, the packing and the excitement before leaving, wasn't it! Creating a pretend campsite holiday at home creates a great deal of security, comfort and confidence—after all, being huddled under a tent with your family is the best feeling.

#WhatYouNeed

↣ **Bedsheets**

↣ **Fairy lights**

↣ **Electric candles**

↣ **A box of games and toys**

↣ **Suitcase**

↣ **Books**

↣ Music system of any kind to play music

↣ Some coloured paper, crayons and pens

↣ Magnets

↣ Glue and tape

↣ Kinetic sand and sand moulds

↣ An old mat

↣ Table and chairs

↣ iPad or laptop (optional)

↣ Blackboard and some chalk (optional)

↣ An inflatable pool or large tub (optional)

#HowtoPrep

✴ Make your own campsite at the beach in your very home to spend some quality time with your children—either in an empty space, a terrace or a backyard.

✴ Take two tables or two high chairs and put them 4–5 feet apart. Tie up a few bedsheets and stretch them over the chairs or the tables. If you are indoors, tie up the middle of the sheet to a hook on the ceiling or a railing (if you are on the terrace). Layer the tent with blankets and put some fairy lights and beanbags around, if possible.

✴ Put a box of your child's favourite books inside the tent.

✴ Place the music system and some stuffed animals outside the tent.

✴ Place an old mat outside with the kinetic sand and some sand moulds (to make sandcastles), buckets, spades, beach balls, etc.

✳ You can keep a laptop or an iPad in the tent for a night-time movie experience.

✳ Draw and colour in fishes in different colours and then stick a small round magnet behind the fishes. Now tie another magnet to a string and tie the string to two pencils (fishing rods). Place the fishes and pencils on a blue mat outside the tent.

✳ Place a small table and a few chairs outside the tent. You can decorate the table with a tablecloth and candles.

#HowtoPlay

✳ Tell your child you are planning a beachside camping trip at home. For that, tell him to gather all the items you require to make it happen and seek his assistance in putting the entire thing together.

✳ Ask him to pack his suitcase with games and toys he would like to use at the camping site.

✳ Now, get dressed—wear your beach attire and go across to your beach campsite. Pack a snack basket with sandwiches, popcorn, chips, granola bars and other snacks you may want to gorge on while at the campsite.

✳ Once you get there, unpack your bags and assemble your items neatly at the campsite.

✳ Read some books, play some games in the tent. Come outside and do some fishing (with the magnetic fish you have made and the pencils to act as fishing rods). Play with the kinetic sand and make some sandcastles. Play some music, dance and do some yoga.

✳ If you have an inflatable pool or a large tub, fill it with water, get into your swimsuit and jump in!

✳ When you are done, play a movie on your iPad or laptop and enjoy your snacks on the picnic table by the candlelight—the perfect end to the perfect holiday. Parents can take an ice-box with some beer or wine, and enjoy their own timeout too!

#KeySkills

☞ Creativity and imagination skills
☞ Social and emotional skills
☞ Behavioural skills
☞ Collaboration and problem-solving skills

15. TEACHER-TEACHER

Playing Teacher-Teacher was always a fun activity when we were young. So why not try it again with our kids and make it more entertaining and informative for them?

#WhatYouNeed

☞ Whiteboard or blackboard or busyboard (busyboard helps to plan things in a more cohesive manner and makes it easier to lay out different activities. To make the busy board you will need—a couple of sheets of paper, coloured pens and some stickers)

☞ A table and a few chairs

☞ A pair of spectacles (for the child to wear on his head) and an outfit that may resemble that of their teacher in school

☞ A stick or a pointer or a ruler

#HowtoPrep

✱ Depending on what your child is learning at school, write or draw four activities on four sheets of paper. For example, it could be the letters of the alphabet on one, numbers on another, sequencing on third, spot-the-difference on fourth.

✱ Cut a circle and put the numbers around it to resemble a clock.

✱ Now make a report card. On one side of a book or notepad, keep a column for students to enter their names and leave another column for the teacher (your child) to enter points.

✱ Set this up on a table and line up chairs for teachers and parents to sit. You can invite other family members too.

✱ Go through the activities with your child and ensure he is able to understand them. A great tip before you begin this play is to tell your child in advance that he should learn specific things this week in order to showcase them the following week in the Teacher-Teacher activity. Spend that week helping and testing him on the concepts he has chosen and that you will put on the busyboard. Ensure that it is something he is comfortable with. With this goal in mind, he is more likely to want to learn, in order for the role-reversal the next week to be successful, where he will need to teach what he has learnt.

#HowtoPlay

✴ Tell your child to announce the curriculum and invite everyone to take their seats in the classroom. He can ask them to bring along their water bottles. Ask your child if you can be his assistant and help him administer the class teaching them the alphabet, the numbers, the time, spot the differences, sequencing etc. (so you can offer suggestions).

✴ Then ask him to inform inform everyone of the topic. Allow him to teach as he deems fit.

✴ Interrupt lightly, as if giving a suggestion, in case they say the wrong thing.

✴ Once the class is over, your child must test the knowledge of the students—he will ask a question and everyone has to answer. Then accordingly, your child will fill in the report card (with your assistance) and give a grade or score to everyone.

✴ Then, it is snack time, and everyone breaks to grab a quick bite.

✴ After the snack time, your child informs everyone of their scores and class is dismissed.

✴ The class meets again the following day or week and then the earlier four activities can be replaced with four new activity pages.

✴ This is great fun to do with family and friends who are curious to know what your child learns at school.

#KeySkills

- ⮞ Cognitive skills
- ⮞ Language development skills and vocabulary
- ⮞ Logical reasoning skills
- ⮞ Alphabet recognition and writing
- ⮞ Number recognition and writing

16. LET'S GO TO THE MOVIES

Is movie night your child's favourite night of the week? Here is an easy way to put them to work to recreate a movie theatre experience in a simple and effective way.

#WhatYouNeed

- ⮞ Five to six sheets of paper
- ⮞ Cardboard box (optional)
- ⮞ Packaged items from your kitchen like candy bars, juice boxes, ketchup, fruit bowls, popcorn, chips, cookies, water bottles, etc.
- ⮞ Bread and cheese or peanut butter or jam or regular butter to make a sandwich (optional)
- ⮞ Colour pens or crayons

#HowtoPrep

* First, let your child arrange some chairs in a row in front of the television. Label the back of the chairs as A1, B2, C3, and so on.

* Then, take your child into the kitchen and ask him to help you make or bring out the snacks and the beverages—popcorn or chips or cookies or candy bars, water bottles, juice, etc. If your child can make something himself, like a sandwich perhaps, let him prepare those.

* Now, we have to make a menu. On a sheet of paper, draw all of the items you have taken out of your kitchen. Let your child get creative in copying the food items—they do not have to be an exact replica. Use Post-it notes to put the same prices on the food items.

* Next, we make the tickets—show your child a picture of a movie ticket and ask them to copy the same. If they need assistance in writing, you can help them with that. Make the number of tickets equivalent to the number of members in the family who will watch the movie. Correspond that with the seat numbers on the back of the chairs, so if there are four members, you can go from A1 to D4. If your child can write, they can even put the person's name or how they are related to your child, on the ticket, like—Mom, Dad, Grandmom and Granddad, etc.

* Once done, set up a snack counter on a table or side table and put out the menu card on it..

✳ If you want to go all out, you can cut open a cardboard box, place it on the table and put up a sign on it that says 'BOX OFFICE'. The tickets can be bought and sold from here.

#HowtoPlay

✳ Your child has to stand at the pretend box office and the family members (include as many people as you can) have to enter one at a time and purchase tickets from the counter and pay the child, the ticket-seller, some money.

✳ Once they have bought the tickets, the people can go to the Snack Counter and the child can read the menu to them. He should ask which snack or beverage they want. Each family member buys the snacks they want, hands over the money to the child and is finally ushered to their seat as per the seat number on the ticket, which your child has to match from the back of seat.

✳ Voila! You have for yourself a great activity and a beautiful movie theatre setting. You can sit back, relax and enjoy a family show or movie.

✳ Read and engage in a discussion on the various jobs involved in the functioning of a cinema hall—from the person at the ticket counter to the cook who makes the food at the food counter to the usher who directs you to your seat and so on.

#KeySkills

↬ Alphabet recognition and writing
↬ Number recognition and writing

- Fine and gross motor skills
- Social and emotional development
- Visual-processing skills

CHAPTER 7

#MomTruthsandMyths

*We all need empty hours in our lives or
we will have no time to create or dream.*
—ROBERT COLES

When I got pregnant, it was not a planned pregnancy—and I am
the kind of person who plans everything in life. I typically have a
five-year plan for my personal life and also one for every venture
I start professionally. I am also the kind of person who likes to be
fully informed and aware, and surprises of any kind are not usually
appreciated. So, I decided to read several books on parenting, attend
parenting seminars and talk to parents of older children about what
their first few years were like. I realized one thing during this phase
of preparation—parenting books often make you feel like a failure
before you have even begun. The guide-type structure makes you
feel inadequate and you wonder if you can keep up with the alleged
parenting 'experts'. Did not breastfeed for a year? Bad Mommy! Used
a pacifier? Uh-oh, you are the easy-way-out Mommy! One-year-
old child still not walking? Slow Mommy! Eighteen-month-old

child still not talking? Judgey-wudgey eyes and raised eyebrow! Showed them the TV or the mobile screen so early? Irreparable damage to the eyes is already done! Left child alone with the nanny? Bad Mommy! Went back to work? Negligent Mommy! Child prefers eating only one kind of food? Oh, well, good luck! You have a fussy eater! Not potty-trained by two years of age? Now your child will never be potty trained! As if there is any adult in the world who cannot manage to go to the bathroom on his own due to delayed potty-training! And the labels and judgments go on and on.

Motherhood does *not* come with a manual and it cannot come with a code, because unlike everything else in the world, this is something so personal and so dependent on your everyday life and personality. Isn't there something positive to be said for mothers who are figuring it out as they go? For the ones who use this process of trial and error where whatever sticks is the winner? No book or guide told me that the way I do things for my child is the best way possible. I do believe in guidelines, but I think they are best developed while parenting and seeing what works for you as a family. There were many techniques I developed to deal with difficult parenting situations and these techniques came about by trying different things and the ones that worked for us became our holy grail. 'If there's a book that you want to read, but it hasn't been written yet, then you must write it,' said the famous writer Toni Morrison. So, I did just that and delved into writing this book—this is not a parenting guide—this is a make-your-moments-with-your-child-fun kind of a book where I have tried to share various processes that I put in place that brought us much joy as parents and helped our child's overall development and contributed to a happy home.

MOM TRUTHS

So, let us start with mom truths that no one tells you before you give birth.

✿ MOM TRUTH 1

No one tells you the truth about breastfeeding. It is by far the strangest phenomenon in the world of motherhood—no part of it as an activity is enjoyable, yet it is the thing that *only* you as the mother can do to meet the needs of your child and *that* makes it beautiful. But no book, documentary, seminar or article on parenting could prepare you for the wide range of emotions and physical pain one goes through during breastfeeding. Mothers are shamed if they did not breastfeed for long enough; they are shamed if they breastfed for too long. Who created the rule about the right number of months that a child must be exclusively breastfed? And who is the controlling authority on it? The amount of time you breastfeed is often talked about as significant as it concerns the overall development and immunity of a child. During my research, I encountered a mother who as a child had been breastfed for sixteen months and yet has been suffering from respiratory conditions and allergies her entire life. There was another woman who was never breastfed due to insufficient supply and she is a hale and hearty forty-year-old today. Similarly, there is substantial research that indicates that the number of months or days a child has been breastfed does not have any direct correlation to their later development. So, there are no universal breastfeeding rules and mothers should not be made to feel badly if they do or do not follow them. If you chose not to breastfeed beyond a few days or a few months for whatever reason, that is your choice. You must do what works for you and be bold and brazen about it. I stopped breastfeeding when my son was almost eight months old because my schedule just did not permit it. I was so tired all the time between work and personal commitments that it had taken a toll on me. I decided then that I could not put myself through it anymore and I simply stopped. And despite the not-so-subtle mom-shaming I received and the fact that I occasionally missed being needed for a feed by my tiny creation, I felt like I had a new lease on life and my life was suddenly in my control again. So, do not judge or allow anyone to judge you. Take control, make a decision that works for your happiness and stick with it.

🌸 MOM TRUTH 2

No one writes about postpartum depression as a by-product of becoming a mother. It is a depression that may or may not be clinical and may or may not require medication, but it is a *rite of passage*, which nobody tells you about or talks about. Why can't you be depressed because you suddenly feel responsible for this tiny being and your life is not yours anymore? Why can't you feel a little lonely because your days are now based on the hunger and other needs of your baby? Why can't you be afraid about the future and how the baby will change your dynamic with your husband and all those around you? Why can't you be upset over your unrecognizable body, which is the primary source of nourishment for your child now? Why can't you be frustrated about the uncertainty of your career? Will you be able to work again? Will you be able to give your full attention to anything again? You can be afraid and you can be depressed, and you can acknowledge it—talk to someone, do something to uplift yourself and deal with all the emotions you are feeling. The word *postpartum* is considered scary and is associated with a deep dark hole you are sucked into, and while others may not experience such difficult emotions to such an extreme, you have the right to feel what you feel. No one wants to admit and tell you it is a rite of passage. Every new mother goes through a gamut of emotions and uncertainties and it is bound to affect her mental health. So, anyone who tells you they did not go through any kind of emotional turmoil, is not being truthful. I wish someone prepared me by saying, 'Go into motherhood fully knowing that you *will* be upset and depressed. You will think at some point that you are nothing more than a milking cow and that may be your identity for a short while. But there is a light at the end of the tunnel and that is worth the ride'. So, today I am telling you this to prepare you for the inevitable.

❀ MOM TRUTH 3

No one tells you about Mom Guilt—something you will deal with for the rest of your life. Everything you do for your child will never be enough and you will not be able to stop second-guessing yourself. You will see mothers around you do more for their child or do things differently for their child, you will see other children behave better than yours, you will see them improve their skills faster than your child does, or be more athletically inclined than yours, and as a mother you will wonder—What did I do wrong? Why can't my child be like that child? Am I a bad mother? The moment those thoughts cross your mind, you have to come back to your child's strengths. For instance, each time I see another child doing something my child has not yet mastered or learnt, initially I would fret and

Mom-guilt would kick in. Now, I smile knowingly. I do this because I know what my child has that the other child may not have. And this is not because I think my child is better than someone else's, it is because each child will have his own strengths and weaknesses. And that special strength (which I call superpower) is you. Each child will pick up traits of his parents and enhance these attributes as he comprehends them. So, what you do around him, talk about in front of him are things that he will know and learn and emulate. My son is a great mix of my husband and I—he has my creativity and my husband's athleticism. He did not inherit my husband's pragmatism and logical thinking. But he is wonderfully creative and comes up with innovative ideas every day to keep himself busy and I would like to believe that he has an entrepreneurial bent of mind. He loves coming to the office with me and helping me at work, and is curious, thoughtful and helpful.

My husband and I live in a nuclear family, so we live life on our terms. We come from different cultures, have different careers, have lived together in two countries and our discussions are liberal and diverse. Therefore, my son is exposed to an environment that is unique. So he will be unique, and have strengths that are different from those of other children, and vice versa. For instance, my son had a play date with a friend who has the same last name as my son. As they were discussing last names, my son revealed that he has two last names—one from his mother and one from his father. His friend insisted that could not be as everyone in his family including his mother has the same last name. So, my son explained innocently, 'My parents say that we need to give respect to both Mommy's and Daddy's families so my Mommy has two last names and so do I.' While this may not be the norm, this was a family rule we made and discussed with him, so when he explained it with such conviction, all my apprehensions faded away. Therefore, every time I see a child who is far more advanced than my son in some field or the other, I bring myself back to such moments when he did me proud and I let go of my Mom guilt. Always remember, you are your child's superpower, so let them into your life and let them understand you better and emulate your good qualities. You can make everything better by focusing on the good.

✿ MOM TRUTH 4

Another thing no one tells you about is the Worry Factor—that you will never ever be worry-free as long as you live after being a mother. Even when your child is old enough, you will still worry about his health, his mental well-being, his nutrition, his company, his work, his finances . . . and the list goes on. When your child has a child, you will worry about your child managing life as a mother or a father and then you will worry when they worry about their child. So, the worry factor, which can sometimes be construed as paranoia is something every mother has to deal with and accept. It is a life-long pursuit and is a situation beyond one's control. The sooner you accept that this is the 'new normal', the more adept you will be in dealing with it.

✿ MOM TRUTH 5

Another thing that you hear about but cannot fathom the extent of is the unselfish and self-sacrificing nature of motherhood that will require you to put yourself last and be completely fine with putting everything in your life on the back-burner for your child. Your heart will break and you will feel like a part of you dies each time your child falls ill or gets injured. This is, again, a major part of parenting that is not easy to deal with. The one thing that one must always remember to get through this is that a happy mother is the crux for raising a happy child. So, doing what makes you happy and taking time out now and then ought to make you a happier and a more content mother.

MOM MYTHS

And now for those mom myths that you hear around town—they are simply not the most accurate depiction of parenting, but you start to believe them at some point in your journey.

MOM MYTH 1

As mentioned above, there are numerous mom truths that we are never told about before we become mothers and we are expected to deal with these harsh truths and smile, laugh and joke with our children and act like everything is normal when there are a million things we have to take care of. So, when Mom guilt kicks in, a knee-jerk reaction of the worried, anxious, guilt-ridden mommy is thinking that the way to be the best parent is to be physically present for your child twenty-four hours a day and to ensure that she is around and can protect her child should anything happen.

When you are pregnant, many people ask you what you are going to do once you have the baby—change careers, quit your job, take a break for a few years—thereby fuelling the thought process that as mothers we need to make ourselves available to our children at all times. Making yourself available to your child twenty-four hours a day is the most misguided aspect of parenting.

I have often said that I consider motherhood a huge blessing and I do feel that my son is an intrinsic part of me. I can feel his every emotion in every fibre of my being. I also am deeply in love with my husband whom I met when I was nineteen and we have been together ever since. However, being a wife and a mother is not enough for me. I have personal aspirations and ambitions and things that I want to achieve in my lifetime and I am finally unapologetic and unabashed about it. I did not want to be the mother who is neglectful of her child and does not have her finger on his pulse; neither did I want to be the mother who is so obsessed with her child's every move and is so available to him that she stifles his independent growth. How does one balance it and get a bit of both worlds? So, the way I saw it was that I have two choices—I can give up on all my dreams and be available to my son and win a fictitious 'Mother of the Year' award (in my mind) but feel unaccomplished and unsatisfied, or I can pursue my dreams slowly but surely, with the same tenacity, if not the same time commitment, and be the best mother possible in my personal capacity. I chose the latter and I do not judge those who chose the former. I stayed at home for a few months and it is much more difficult to be a stay-at-home mom than it is to be a working mother, because as a working mom, you come home invigorated and ready to spend the rest of the day with your child whereas a stay-at-home mom is with them all the time. But at the same time, as a working mother, mom guilt is something that eats away at you and you deal with constant mom-shaming. It took me a long time, but I have made my peace with the fact that I cannot be available physically and at all times for my child but he is always on my mind and if I was needed, I would be there in a heartbeat.

✿ MOM MYTH 2

Research indicates that whether you chose to work or stay at home, being available to your child at every second of the day reduces their self-reliance, their independence and their ability to problem-solve. There are colossal benefits that your child can derive by merely playing alone in his room. If you are available all the time, he will not be inclined to do so and you become his sole source of entertainment, which as a mother you may enjoy but eventually you will begin to lose sight of yourself and your sole identity will be that of a mom, and it will not make your child self-dependent. It happens to the best of us. To break free, take up something that will take your mind off your child, house, husband and family, and engage yourself intellectually, mentally, physically or creatively. Staying busy and focused, and doing something for YOURSELF will not be stress-free, it will be challenging. But nothing worth attaining in this world comes free or easy.

It could be a work-out regime, yoga, a book club, a course you always wanted to take—whatever it is, do it if it gives you a sense of self-worth outside of your family. People derive self-worth in many ways—as long as there is something that you are doing that feeds your soul, you will be a happier mother. When I went back to work when my son was six-months-old, for a few hours daily, I would be lying if I said I was not paranoid and worried and did not feel guilty about leaving him, but at the same time I felt a sense of achievement. The world was suddenly conquerable and I felt if I could manage my work and my son, I was invincible and there was nothing I could not do. There was a renewed sense of self-confidence. I gave up my life as a lawyer and instead started multiple businesses so I could manage my own hours. It was not easy and you need a steady support system to get you through it. But it is achievable, if you put your mind to it and if you really want it. It is not the number of hours you spend with your child but what you do together in those few hours that will define his growth and his behaviour in the hours that you are not around.

✻ MOM MYTH 3

Another misguided aspect of parenting is that co-sleeping is the best way to maintain a bond with your child. I personally do not subscribe to this. Once in two weeks, we do a movie night and our son is allowed to sleep in our room, and of course also when he is unwell. But co-sleeping is a strict no-no. I resolutely believe that independence needs to be inculcated from the onset and sleeping in separate rooms and allowing your child to put himself to bed is of utmost importance. While one school of thought believes that co-sleeping helps soothe a child, gives them less emotional stress and helps increase their bond with the parents, I am of the alternative school of thought and of the firm belief that the bond with a parent can be cultivated in several more constructive ways (many are spelled out in this book). Besides, I do not know many mothers who slept well next to their child all night. I would wake up every five minutes with every stir and would not be able to function properly (or at all) the next day. A well-rested mom is crucial to the very existence of a healthy child. Of the many selfless things that mothers do, co-sleeping ought not be one of them.

There are many 'rules' in parenting—you need to breastfeed for a fixed number of months; avoid any form of screen time; don't give

SHOUGER MERCHANT DOSHI

your child anything with sugar or refined flour; don't give the bottle too early; don't give the bottle too late; start a new language at age five; introduce a new food every week and the list goes on. These rules are subjective and arbitrary, and need not be followed. There is a lot to be said about choosing the right path at the right time for you and your child. If you need a few hours off mom duty and that is what is important for you at that time, put on that movie for your child so you can get some rest. If breastfeeding is taking its toll on you, weigh that against your child's needs and introduce formula when you think the time is right—not because the world is telling you it is not time yet. Do what is right for you, your child and your family as a unit and don't feel ashamed about it.

Research indicates that as a child grows, moms take up certain extracurricular activities and sign their children up for classes and events because 'all the other moms are doing it'. But every child is different and sometimes you child won't like the most popular music class and you will feel like he is missing out; but instead, if you look deep enough you will see he is interested in dance or chess or some other sport. Recognizing your child's inclination from a young age can help hone them, support them and allow them to flourish. Sometimes, it is okay to go against the grain (forgo that rat race) and follow your child's strengths.

So, mommies, regardless of whether you bought into the mom truths or the myths, remain confident in your personal abilities and your wonderfully unique and distinctly gifted child. Most importantly, do not lose yourself completely in parenting. There are some things for your child and he will have that and eventually grow up and fly the coop, but the things you do for yourself stay so that nest is never empty.

CHAPTER 8

#HighConflictSituations

'In order for children to learn how to do hard things, you have to let them go through hard times. There is no way to truly master something without experiencing it.'

—SARA BEAN

No one ever tells you about the high conflict situations and the various tantrums you will encounter as your child grows. Through trial and error, I have somewhat managed to make these high conflict situations enjoyable, and I want to share my secrets through this series of mommy hacks.

❋ MOMMY HACK 1—BEDTIME DRAMA

There is no such thing as a perfect mom; I, for one, am far from one. That said, my son has slept from 7:30 p.m. to 7:30 a.m. since he was six months old and people often ask me which secret sauce do I feed him to maintain this routine. I firmly believe in a routine—it is the only thing that can give you a set amount of hours with your child after class or school, an early dinner and enough time to cuddle and do your bedtime rituals, after which you can relax, unwind, have an uninterrupted conversation with your husband, have your dinner in peace and maybe even a glass of wine, read a good book or watch a good movie. So, how did I do it? This method I have employed is foolproof, but requires early adoption. *It is a combination of pretend play, stories and a semi-rigid routine.* From the time my son was one and a half years old and showed a keen interest in books and stories, I would make up stories to tell him every night, like any other parent. But the made-up stories involved the very same protagonists—Jolly, the giraffe, who consistently ate the leaves off all the trees in the city; Zoey, the zebra, who lived in the jungle near the city and a boy named Ronald who could morph into a frog sometimes. They had many adventures together, and every night, I would narrate to my son only one chapter of my self-concocted story and trail off to continue it the next night. So, because the story never ended and was left on a cliff-hanger the previous night, he was excited about bedtime the next evening and was happy to jump into his bed and hear about what happened next to his characters whom he knew better than I did. The story did not end till he was four years old, which is when I realized I had been doing this for over two years and I had to now find something different to excite him with. And that is when we started to take up one pretend play activity every weekend, for which we would prepare the entire week.

For example, if we are going to build a construction site on the weekend, we read up on that concept, found out all we can about the topic, gathered the materials and discussed it every night before going to bed. The planning got him excited for the execution stage (which will not happen till the weekend). So, we could discuss it all week and were able to get him to bed on weeknights) and hence, he used to go to bed on time because he wanted to wake up and start planning for the activity the next day.

However, this would not be possible without the enforcement of a semi-stringent routine when it comes to meals and bedtimes. Once that is in place, this method can prove to be pretty useful. Take up a concept that you can discuss throughout the week, every week, and then build a story around it. You may read a book about it and then engage your child in an activity that involves some reading or writing based on the concept or something that exercises his motor skills. This will not only allow him to comprehend the concept properly, but also explore it for himself. Always have a wind-down period before it's lights-out time. On weekends, there may be an extra hour of play, but on school nights, it is non-negotiable. If you try this method with a dose of excitement and an ounce of firmness, it does wonders for your uninterrupted sleep and your child's sleep patterns.

🐾 MOMMY HACK 2—MEALTIME MADNESS

How to feed a cranky toddler from a nutritious array of healthy foods is a well-kept secret by the universe and no mother can seem to crack it. I am no exception to the rule. They say you must eat the rainbow, and the more colours in your food, the better. But children like consistency. I plan the food menu for the week ahead of Sunday, and every Sunday I try to think of novel ways to introduce healthy and new foods into my child's existing set of meals (by camouflage) that he likes. Sometimes he catches it, and sometimes he does not. But he has to eat what has been made for him. There is no other choice. Just like Mommy and Daddy have to eat what has come out of the kitchen for them. If it is a really cranky day, use a system of rewards or loss of privileges to coax him into eating. Much like life, persistence is the one important quality needed for successful food introduction. However many times you try and fail, if you stay the course, you will eventually succeed because your child will get tired of protesting and eventually bite (quite literally) the bullet, so don't give up. It is also important to have consistency in terms of where you eat every day and what your child is doing during mealtimes. If it is a weekday, we discuss our day and work, we ask him about his school and about specific friends or teachers and get him to converse with us while he eats his meal.

A feeling of togetherness during mealtimes is a *must*. This is unsettling for many parents because they want to spend mealtimes talking to each other because they have not seen their spouse all day and there are always things to discuss and catch up about. This can take some getting used to, but this is the best time to converse with each other as a family. Dinner table conversations are a great way to find out more about your child because they are casual in nature. It is also important to include your child in your discussion with your husband and ask him what his opinions are, even if you are not going to take them into consideration. They appreciate the validation and get enthusiastic about it and this goes a long way in building their confidence. Another reason parents miss dinner time with their children is their timing. However, we eat at 7 p.m. with our son, which pre-motherhood was unheard of. And while there are days where I cannot wait for my son to go to bed so I can have a conversation with my husband, I also realize the importance of the spontaneous conversations we have about the world with our son, which exposes him to a richer understanding of various concepts and enhances his vocabulary.

On weekends, some leeway can be provided. Lunchtime could be spent reading a book or listening to an audiobook. I have found this has given much focus and concentration to mealtime and it has helped cultivate an interest in books and stories. To imagine a story involves a deeper level of curiosity and vision, and keeps children engrossed and focused on the story rather than on the food on the table. And when there is a particularly unappetizing vegetable nesting on your child's plate, it can become more palatable when he is engrossed in his favourite Netflix show.

I found the use of books and stories useful to expose my child to the idea that a specific food is not dangerous, formidable or intimidating. It comes in handy if your child refuses certain foods and does not want to try them. For instance, my son had a particular aversion to salads and would not even look in their direction. Since my son was getting his greens in different forms, I paused all efforts to get him to try it. One day, we were reading a book from the *Pete the Cat* series where all the dinosaurs try a salad for the first time and find it delicious. After reading that book, he kept asking me for a salad, but I thought he was merely joking. One day I decided to fix him one and he lapped it up, and I was thrilled to have a salad buddy for lunch. After that, I tried to resort to books that introduced and explored specific foods in a casual way and made them less daunting and even appetizing (dare I say) to a child.

✖ MOMMY HACK 3–HOMEWORK HATRED

Schoolwork, homework and anything that ends with 'work' is not easy to extract from a child. However, I found it easier to make homework fun by putting in place a pretend race and using a system of rewards and loss of privileges. First, the homework space must be one you set up with your child, taking their inputs and making it an area so nice that he really wants to use it, but can only use it for homework. Next, the timing for homework must be the same daily, but it must be after a round of prolonged play and not directly after school or a class. Third, start by approaching the topic lightly by joking with him. For instance, ask if you can fit into something of his you like and watch him laugh at the thought of it. Be playful, play some music, sing his favourite song, play a game and let him win and then say, 'Oh, we have played so much and you kept winning. Now let me beat you in your homework!' He takes his worksheet out and I take out another one; I go to another room and peep in on him now and then. He thinks this is a race and finishes his homework quickly. Once I compare our worksheets, I tell him I did not get half as much done as him and he is too smart for Mommy. Sometimes, we do a race to finish the homework before Daddy comes home or before a play date or before the song finishes. When it is couched as a game, they enjoy it far more. Another thing that helps is to review the daily or weekly schedule together and remind your child of the fun things you have planned for the weekend—a play date, a swim, an outing, a birthday party, a pretend play activity—and remind him that the fun begins only once the homework is over. Say things like, 'We can discuss that movie you have wanted to watch after the homework for the weekend is done,' or 'Rey is waiting to play with you, but he has finished his homework. So, let us finish ours so playtime can begin.' Sometimes it also helps to ask what they feel like doing. If there are choices in the homework, let him select what he wants to do. This is a great way to show him respect and eliminate the coercive nature of homework, which will make him rebel less. Giving rewards, praise and recognition also goes a long way in making him view homework positively. Say to your husband loud and clear so your child can hear, 'You have no idea how quickly and how well he did his homework today. He is so very smart.' This helps in associating positive vibes with the homework and encourages them to do it better the next day to show off to you again. Further, it always helps to explain the trajectory to him so he can see the bigger picture. For example, when my son comes to work with me and asks questions about what I do and how I do it, I often tell him, 'Mommy went to school and studied very hard, then Mommy went to college and studied hard there too, then Mommy went to university and studied there too and that is how Mommy was able to realize what she likes to do and then she could start her own business. Going to school and doing homework is a great way of finding what you like to do and what you are good at.' Children understand more than we know and the more consistently we enforce these habits, it forms a part of their routine and the protests will decrease over time and the power struggle will be eliminated.

✱ MOMMY HACK 4—'BATH IS BAD' SYNDROME

Bath time should be a fun, soothing experience and not a hectic, unhappy one as it is in most households. The way to shake it up and ensure your child enjoys it and laughs through it is to add the much-needed element of fun to it. First, try and use bubbles, bath colour, music in the background, bath toys, coloured lights, glow in the dark soap, finger painting, water balloons, ice cubes and much more to entice your little one into a lovely bathing experience. You can place several vessels of different sizes and shapes in the bathroom, which can be used to fill and pour water. Feel free to use objects such as a sieve or a spatula from the kitchen that will enable his motor skills while he plays. Also, make lathering the soap fun—create soapy water and make the process of scrubbing himself a race. This will eventually teach him to bathe independently. Second, try putting a mirror in the bathroom so your child can make funny faces and entertain himself while bathing and have a laugh. Sometimes, he can race his collection of fishes or other animals, cars and figurines, and other times he can put up a puppet show. But make sure you, or whoever is bathing them, is talking to them and giving them heads up about when it is time to put water on their head, near their eyes, etc. to keep them comfortable and safe, and establish their trust in you during bath time. Finally, talk about how you gain a superpower by having a bath—you get rid of the bad guys (germs) and you smell great and your skin and body stay healthy. These are some amusing ways to make bath time a fun adventure and not just another item on the agenda that has to be ticked off or an area of friction.

What I learned the hard way was that when you approach these high conflict areas with an attitude of making it fun, it is not so overwhelming or stressful anymore.

CHAPTER 9

#HouseRules101

Culture arises and unfolds in and as play.
—JOHAN HUIZINGA

I read somewhere, 'Being a parent is like folding a fitted sheet. No one really knows how.' I could not agree more. It is a daily struggle to make decisions—Should I be tough? Should I give in? Should I negotiate? Will I be judged? And almost each day ends with, 'Gosh, I feel so guilty' about something or the other.

It is literally a plethora of emotions that a parent goes through daily! And there is no escaping this pandemonium because not only is each parent different, each child is unique too and reacts in different ways to a parent's temperament. But parenting cannot always be child-led. There are some procedures that I encountered through a process of elimination that I sincerely believe are essential to enforce because they help inculcate a modicum of discipline in unpredictable toddlers and lead to better habits if adopted early.

There are the twenty-five house rules that I stuck to in order to parent my child through his toddler years and all the tantrums, that may help you if you subscribe to a similar school of thought:

1. ***Stick to a routine like your life depends on it***: This is the primary secret of easy parenting. I tell moms all the time that maintaining a schedule and enforcing it in your life as well as your child's life is 80 per cent of the battle won. But somehow, not many follow it. Pen down a schedule that works for you and inform everyone in the house about it. Put up a calendar in the kitchen, your child's room, your office and your room, if needed. My schedule ensures that the morning routine of bath, breakfast, and getting ready for school is all done before 7 a.m., so we have twenty minutes before the school bus arrives to have a chat, read a book and so on. Once he is back from school, he has a snack and some downtime after which we have structured play, so in that hour, he can choose to do anything that involves tactile stimulation such as building blocks, Magna-tiles or sand activities. Following that, is active hour where he can go downstairs or to a garden or on a play date and run around, skate, play football, hide and seek, etc. After that we can do art and craft or play family board games, followed by dinner, bath and bedtime reading. Bedtime is always at the same time every day. There can be leeway given in a lot of parenting rules, but keeping a semi-rigid schedule is a must. The schedule must remain malleable because things change every day in a child's life and one day if they do not want to do tactile stimulation activities, they can bake instead or read for an extra hour. However, the routine of the day must

remain unaffected. There are many scientific advantages to following a semi-rigid routine in the house:

a) It keeps your child calm because he knows exactly what to expect and what is coming next.

b) It establishes healthy and constructive habits.

c) It helps him fall into a great sleep schedule.

d) It gives him a sense of security, so he can take charge of his activities and duties.

e) It eliminates the negotiations and the power struggles and ultimately leads to a happier childhood.

It is also important not to overschedule or stifle creativity while maintaining this schedule. So, allow your child to lead his day as long as the overall schedule is not compromised and mealtime and bedtime remain unchanged. Children love being involved in the schedule, so sometimes my son and I set the schedule together for the week and that allows him some control over his own routine and enables him to be prepared every step of the way. I swear by this guideline: a good schedule + the inculcation of good habits = a conducive atmosphere for good behaviour.

2. *Be a parent, not a friend*: I always loved watching those movies where the mom and daughter were best friends and did everything together. But the reality is that when your child is young, they are looking to you for direction. If you are their friend and play along, you will not be able to set them straight when it is needed. Being firm comes with the territory, but there are many ways to do that while being compassionate. If I have to be firm with my son, I first explain to him what he did wrong and I inform him that

he gave me no choice and that it hurts me to be angry with him because I love him so much. But rules are not meant to be broken and what he did was wrong. If he shouts, screams and cries, I hug him till he is calm and then explain why I am angry with him and what the repercussions of his actions are. Instead of 'cry it out', I 'hug it out'. But words always hurt more than actions. So, I will show him that I love him even though I am upset. I will say things like 'I am very upset because of the hurtful nature of what you said to me. So I cannot talk to you for a few minutes.' This is more effective on a child than yelling, screaming or threatening to banish them. Keep your approach firm, consistent yet loving always.

3. ***Communication should be a priority***: Communicating with your child is a top priority. Tell them what you did all day, involve them in your life, tell them about your work, your friends, your likes and dislikes. You will be surprised at the level of understanding your child has for various situations in your life if you just talk about them with him. Further, children learn by observation and enjoy mimicking behaviour. The way you speak, the language and the vocabulary you use, etc. go a long way in shaping their personalities. Tell them about the first time you met your child's father or stories about their grandparents or about a holiday you took that was memorable. Tell them the meaning behind the words you use. Read a passage to them from the book you are reading. Explain the reasons behind the choices you have made in life. You may think they do not understand these things, but they do and every step you take is being watched and observed. So, converse

with them and get them to be on the same page as you and understand you better as a parent and a person. Even when any unpleasant things happen in your child's life, they should know they can talk to you about it. If you hear your child has hit someone on the playground, your immediate reaction should not be to yell at him and tell him this cannot happen again. Ask him why he did that. Ask about what he felt at the time. Then you can tell him, 'I understand you were angry. It is okay to be angry and frustrated. But hitting another child or anyone else is not good behaviour. What you could do next time, is simply tell that person that what he did made you angry and upset and I am sure that he would understand.' Communication is key in making parenting easier.

4. *Break gender stereotypes*: It may be a man's world, but a child should grow up believing it is not one and be able to envision what it can be. Beware of the labels and clichés a child is exposed to while growing up. Do not be the parent who does blue for the boy and pink for the girl. Mix it up a little bit. Let them be drawn to what attracts them, regardless of gender, age, religion, etc. My son once told me that he wanted to go to the toy store but we would have to wait for Dad to get home to drive him to the store. When I offered to drive him, he did not believe I could drive because I had not driven him anywhere in a while. He wondered if it was just a boy-thing. To allay his doubts, I took him for a long drive. It is important to show your child that both Mommy and Daddy can do almost anything. Beat the gender stereotypes by doing things like playing football, managing gadgets around the house,

attempting to fix his toy, etc. as a mother, and as a father, you could cook and do the laundry now and then. It does not matter if you do not succeed but the fact that you tried goes a long way. Show your child your work or pictures of things you have done in the past. Explain how important it is that both Mommy and Daddy work—not just to secure a better future for him, but also because it gives you a great deal of happiness and a sense of fulfillment. They need to understand that both parents have an essential part to play in their upbringing and while Mommy may look different than Daddy, both are equally important.

5. *Talk to your child like he is an adult*: Baby talk has not done a great deal for any child. Speak to your child as if he is an adult. Explain things to him as you would to anyone else, even if he does not understand them. He will learn and pick up things from you that you could never imagine, but only if he is treated with respect and not trivialized as a child. He will feel like he is a part of the family and a part of its great joys and challenges.

6. *Never measure your child's worth by someone else's standards*: Some children learn to walk later than others, some learn to talk before others, some don't crawl and start walking straightaway. When it is your child that has not yet started reading, writing or counting as per the 'developmental milestones' that the so-called experts have marked, you as a parent will feel like a complete failure. The important thing to remember is that your child may be late to some parties, but he will still show up. Nurture the unique qualities your child has—whether it is their inclination for music, an excellent recall, great social skills, athletic skills or a creative

bent of mind, etc.—and celebrate those, because other children may not have that potential yet. Create a bond with your child based on what their skill set is and do not force them to be anyone else. Whenever you feel like other children are doing something your child cannot yet do, focus on the things your child can do well and you will be a happier mother. Every child is unique and has something special to offer. This took me some time to accept but the minute I realized my son's strengths, I intentionally nurtured them further; I refrain from measuring him against any other child.

7. *Inculcate habits*: Children love being a part of the family and engaging in its various daily activities. Simple things like putting toys away, folding clothes, bringing you a glass of water, laying the table, etc. can be made fun for the child. Telling your child, 'I am so excited for tomorrow. I have planned a great activity for us. We are going to fold clothes together while listening to your favourite soundtrack from *Lion King*,' works better than, 'Help me fold the clothes; I don't want to do all the chores myself.' Another tip: Never call it a chore. We call them 'responsibilities' and each one of us has them; shirking your responsibilities means you have to do more the next day.

8. *Praise effort, not victory*: When your child attempts something, even if it does not turn out as expected—praise it like it is the best thing in the world. Build their self-esteem and their confidence while praising them, so they do not shy away and continue to try and do better.

9. *Have family rituals*: Always have certain rituals that you do together as a family every day—a physical activity, a board

game, a card game, reading, yoga, baking, cooking, etc. We bake and engage in one pretend play activity together once a week. We also cuddle in bed together and read a bedtime story for fifteen minutes before it is bedtime. Setting time aside for these rituals leads to building your child's social and emotional skills.

10. *Apologize when necessary*: If you flare up at your child (and do not worry, it happens to the best of us), there is no harm in apologizing. We are constantly apologizing to our son for yelling at him and he smiles at us. We also expect the same in return from him when he misbehaves. Treating them with respect and as an adult will only garner the same respect for you.

11. **Let your child see the love and respect you have for your partner**: This is really important. A child wants to be in a safe and loving environment. Parents bickering at each other (again, it happens to the best of us) can have an unsettling effect on a child. Even if you fight and make up, make sure your child also sees the making up and the love that you both have for each other. Remember to tell your child when he is going to bed that now it is Mommy and Daddy's time to hang out. It is important that your child is aware that there is 'adult time' for his parents. Mommy and Daddy need to spend some time together too.

12. **Trust your 'momstinct'**: No one knows your child like you do, so if you sense something is off or he is not quite his usual self, chances are you are probably right. Go with that gut feeling and try to pry it out of him—it could be an incident at school or something someone said. But go at it in a casual and nonchalant way. Children are extremely

sensitive and can sense if you are coming on too strong, or are stressed out or anxious.

13. *Do not allow disrespect to become a pattern*: If your child is disrespecting you, don't laugh it off or shrug it off. Deal with it right then and there, so it does not happen again. If you have to be firm, raise your voice or ignore him for a short while—or whatever works in your case—do it, just as long as he realizes he cannot disrespect you again. Bad words cannot be a part of the repertoire and bad behaviour must be called out, so it is not repeated.

14. *Give them responsibility and control at times*: Giving your child certain responsibilities and control over certain things in the house or in their schedule makes them feel more secure about their place in the house; it also makes them more disciplined and happier. Give them the responsibility of laying the table, folding their own clothes, cleaning up their room, helping with putting away your own work items, etc. We use a responsibility chart (part of a game also offered by my company, The Story Merchants, but you can easily make this at home too) where we dole out small sums of money for each 'responsibility' carried out. His responsibilities include regular chores around the house, greeting elders, eating on his own, sleeping on his own, caring for our dog, etc. Money given out is collected in 'Save', 'Spend' and 'Share' envelopes. We teach delayed gratification by collecting in the 'Save' envelope—achieving a long-term goal, like an item that is expensive and requires weeks of 'responsibilities' to collect the requisite amount. Immediate gratification or short-term goals are easily achieved by completing less responsibilities and the item

can be purchased from the 'Spend' envelope. And finally, for 'Share'—we donate 5 per cent of the proceeds earned together to any charitable establishment or it can be used to buy food boxes for the needy.

The Responsibility Chart is something that has worked for us. We found it fun, while our son treated it as a race to finish his chores so he could earn the money with which he could go to a store and buy something he wanted and feel proud of buying with his own hard-earned money. We found that it instilled a love for giving in our child. Providing for the less fortunate is an important attribute for holistic growth. We did the chart for six months and since then, all the responsibilities have become a well-formed habit and are built into his daily schedule. Every action (or inaction) has a consequence for us as adults. This must be taught early. When you do not meet a deadline at work, there is an unfortunate consequence to that. Similarly, if a child does not complete his homework, go to bed on time or eat his meal, he can also get minus points on the Reward Chart, which eventually may impact his desired outcome (which could be anything on his wish list, from more screen time to a specific outing or a toy or a game).

15. *Don't stress about mom guilt:* It is a disease that all moms suffer from. There is no cure and no reprieve. The only way to manage it is to manage your expectations and learn to take a break when you need it. My husband and I travel abroad once a year for two weeks without our son because that is our time to rekindle our love for each other and live life freely. Absence makes the heart grow fonder, and after a few days apart, we cannot wait to return to our son.

Do what you need to do to take that break—whether it is a date night or a weekend alone or roping in nannies and grandparents. It is your right to get some downtime. Remember that your purpose in life extends beyond being the dutiful mommy.

16. *Be a good role model*: The experts say one should lead by example, but this is difficult to do when you are being watched twenty-four hours a day. There will be moments where you will curse, bicker, scream, yell or behave in an uncharacteristic fashion—all of this is a part of being a parent. You cannot be perfect all the time, and your child will love you for being your true and authentic self. And during the times you do falter, catch and correct yourself—if you screamed, apologize and say, 'It is not good to yell, but today Mommy was tired and had a lot of work to do, so she lost her temper. It happens. But I'll try for it to not happen again.' Parents are not infallible; we are human too. Your child can see that you also make mistakes and continue to work on yourself just as he does daily. You are their greatest superhero and you are their greatest influencer. If you are going to tell your child to be kind every day—lead by example and show them the meaning of kindness. If you are going to tell your child to read, then you need to show them the joy that you experience from reading a good book. Everything you do is being emulated.

17. *Listen to your child*: Many parents tend to talk down to their child much more than they talk to them. If you are having a conversation, it cannot be one-sided, so hear them out first before jumping to conclusions or speaking to them or yelling at them. Listen to what they are saying and then

stop, sit back, assess how to respond and then respond. This was by far the best parenting rule I made and have followed.

18. *Do not mollycoddle*: As a parent, often our first reaction is to jump in and save our child—from an untied shoelace to packing their bag to fixing them lunch to finally fighting all their battles for them. Remember, as parents, we cannot always be with our child at all times, so our goal is to help them learn problem-solving skills, not to solve all their problems for them. Through pretend play, we can try to equip them with the resolve and the determination to do things for themselves. This, I must admit, was difficult for me, because I was a rather impatient person and if I saw my son struggle, I often wanted to do it for him. But motherhood requires all kinds of patience and not mollycoddling my child has brought about a positive change in my parenting style. So, sit back and let them face challenges head-on, and only interfere if it is required. Give your child a chance to take on his problems and you may be surprised by what he can say and do.

19. *Get down and dirty:* If your child wants to jump in muddy puddles, do it with him. Unleash the inner child in you who is waiting to emerge. If your child wants to have a race, race him. If your child wants to dress up as a unicorn, do it with him. Let him feel that you are also a playmate in addition to being a parent.

20. *Say 'I love you' and hug and kiss them 1,00,00,000 times a day*: Some days are difficult for us as mothers; we have innumerable things on our minds from family to house to work to finances to school, and keeping up with everything

is a daunting task. So even if you are feeling blue and you have played 'bad cop' all day, never forget to hug and kiss your child a million times and remind them they are loved, because in spite of all the tough love we sometimes need to give, they need to know how loved they are and how we will always do our best for them. Sometimes, it just needs to be said and felt.

21. *Encourage quiet time alone in their playzone:* Children learn a great deal from playing by themselves. Setting up an area in the house where they can play, with enough activities, toys and games that challenge them, is the best way to encourage solo time. It gives them time to explore things and conceptualize them in different ways and use different items in combination with each other. Even sitting and flipping through the images in a book can engage them creatively and allow for logical processing of the images, letters and picture-reading. Children also need to realize that while parents can be playmates, they cannot be there all the time. So, when left to themselves, they need to find innovative ways to engage themselves and as a result develop a sense of independence, confidence and self-reliance that helps build their character. It also encourages unaccompanied problem-solving, which is an essential component of intellectual development. For instance, once I started encouraging solo play in my son's room, he decided he would use that time to make inventions. He would put together various items and make a larger creation and then present it to us at dinnertime. For example, he would rearrange the furniture to make a horse carriage, take a few sticks and strings and tie them together to make a fishing

rod, use his blocks and tiles to make a weapon of some sort, etc. This process of creation and innovation excited him and gave him a huge amount of confidence in his abilities, and he realized he didn't need to keep asking for help to put something together. Independent play also helps them problem-solve and be a leader in school activities.

22. **Read lots of books and play games together as a family:** If you just get an hour with your child in the day, read together and play board games. Board games soothe children, it teaches them collaboration, competition, focus, resilience and teamwork. They are a great bonding activity between parents and children, and not only foster social independence but also sharpen a child's visual recognition and decision-making skills. Teach your child that it is less important to win or lose, but more important to play the game to the best of his ability and to enjoy the process.

23. **Love yourself:** Parenting is a job. It is an unpaid and strenuous job. While it has its rewards—the challenges can drain you. Treat yourself like the Mom Boss that you are because, trust me, for your child, no one can do it better than you. So, love yourself and celebrate yourself from time to time and make sure to tell your whole family that you need 'me time' and explain to your child that you need some time to check out, do something fun for yourself and rejuvenate your mind.

24. **Give value to important people and places:** There are many people and things we value in life, but we do not always express it. Make it a point to tell your child who your close friends are, show him pictures of his cousins who live far away and ensure that you mention important people who

he may not be well-acquainted with or whose memories are not fresh in his mind. Your child will treat your friends and family members the way you treat them or speak about them. So, if you want to foster a good relationship between your child and your friends and family, convey their importance in your life to your child. Talk about them. He will give value to anything you give value to. We live in a digital age where distance is easily overcome by various modes of communication, so we can use these modes to ensure he knows who our loved ones are (near or far) and observe us as we treat them with love and respect.

25. *Pretend play, every week*: Finally, playful parenting is a healthy and nourishing form of parenting. It will keep you and your child happier, more secure, confident and ensure a robust bond between you all as a family. For this, pretend play is one of the most rewarding exercises you can indulge in with your child.

CHAPTER 10

#VocabularyFocus

Reading maketh a full man; conference a
ready man; and writing an exact man.
—Francis Bacon

I have always believed that a rich vocabulary is a gift that keeps on giving. If there is one thing in the world you should do for your child, it should be to boost literacy and enhance your child's glossary of words and phrases. While this learning continues throughout your child's life, there is considerable research to support the belief that an early exposure to words, phrases and worldly concepts helps influence the child's thinking and how well they will understand the spoken and written word in the future.

An important and noteworthy study that took place in 2012, which has become a barometer in measuring the impact of vocabulary on a child's learning process, was one conducted by Meredith Rowe, an educational psychologist. She studied the vocabulary of fifty young children when they were eighteen to fifty-four months of age, in terms of the amount (quantity) and type (quality) of words the parents used with their children. She found certain factors that contributed to a child's vocabulary one year later, such as the parents' education and the child's previous vocabulary. Here are some highlights of her research:

* A child's vocabulary at thirty months was influenced by the quantity of words the parents used. This means that children aged twelve to twenty-four months benefit from being exposed to an increased number of words.

* Children's vocabulary at forty-two months was influenced by parents' use of a variety of sophisticated words. Children aged twenty-four to thirty-six months were able to imbibe and use more varied and complex words and phrases.

* Children's vocabulary at fifty-four months was influenced by parents' conversations. Children aged thirty-six to fifty-four months benefit from conversations about things that happen around them, things that they see, and then they pick up certain words from their parents' responses to daily situations.

The study highlighted that over time, it was not just quantity, but *quality* that was of utmost importance, especially for children aged two years and above, which affected early brain development. Many studies have also highlighted the positive impact of adult interaction on vocabulary and oral language development. Hence, it is imperative that parents closely engage with their children, have in-depth conversations with them, build their communication skills and expose them to multiple situations, places, people and experiences that would lead to introduction of more and more words and phrases that would become a part of their reserve.

But why, you may ask, is having a good vocabulary or a command over language an important cornerstone for early development?

✳ First, there are various aspects of life that a rich vocabulary can teach you. In the early years, simple things such as worldly and cultural concepts, synonyms and antonyms, procedures (shapes, numbers, directions, spatial prepositions {under, above, on}, patterns, rhymes, time, comparative use of words), greetings, identification of sentence classification into categories and sub-categories, which is important to comprehend and cogently construct sentences, as well as to be able to have a basic conversation with peers. The more complex the category or concept that your child understands, the better they are able to process the world and the better their learning curve will be.

✳ Second, it gives your child the ability to articulate what they feel. With an extensive lexicon to describe what they feel, they can be more explicit in communication, which can be a boon for every parent. You can rest assured knowing your child will be able to explain exactly how they feel or what they underwent or share something that made them happy or sad or uncomfortable without thinking twice.

✳ Third, your child will not be stumped while speaking with children older than him. Vocabulary is the foundation for grasp and perception with respect to communication and understanding. The more your child knows how to articulate his thoughts and feelings in words, the easier it will be for him to also understand what others are saying.

✳ Fourth, the better vocabulary your child has at their fingertips, the more advanced their knowledge base is as they are then able to grasp more information.

✳ Fifth, a good vocabulary leads to increased self-esteem, self-reliance and confidence. Your child will automatically assume a healthy intellectual pride in their abilities, which will do wonders for his sense of self-worth. This really helps to compensate for other areas or subjects at school or college where your child may suffer, but his verbal abilities will help him excel in language-based classes, debates, speeches, drama, etc. He would gain recognition through these areas, thereby mitigating the loss of self-confidence due to his weaknesses.

✳ Sixth, good literacy skills and an extensive vocabulary have a definite and proven relationship with the accomplishment of higher educational goals. Pioneering research has demonstrated that having advanced vocabularies of different languages in the early years led to greater educational achievement in the middle years of primary school. Several studies in the last fifteen years have also supported the same hypothesis; there is indeed a correlation between those who have a rich vocabulary and academic and professional achievement.

Whether it is an application for college, a job interview, a presentation, a meeting, a conference, a sales pitch or other events and situations, your child will have an advantage over others; he will be able to fluently communicate, impress, negotiate, advocate and make headway—all due to your engagement and encouragement during his early learning period.

⁕ Seventh, when your child is a reader, he has had exposure to a varied collection of books and therefore has an opulent vocabulary. He will then be able to make informed decisions and formulate opinions based on the knowledge he gathers from those books or even from the conversations with other people. This will provide him clarity on what is right and wrong. He will determine his likes and dislikes. He will comprehend the kind of people he wants to surround himself with. He will also have a better understanding of his capabilities, his role in various situations and how to deal better with people. It is this self-awareness that will take him far in life and help him assess and analyse various situations and problem-solve independently as per his judgement.

So, how can we build our child's vocabulary? Through my research, I formulated some guidelines that I see as having long-term benefits:

⁕ *Discussions and Conversations*: The most important part of parenting is to involve your child in many kinds of discussions and conversations. These could be in relation to the house, your work, your career, familial relationships or other topics. It is a good idea to involve them in your day-to-day life not just to make them feel included, but also to increase their knowledge about various ideas and worldly concepts.

⁕ *Reading*: When I was younger, I was a voracious reader and read a book a day, sometimes even two. I read everything that they said I was too young for. I devoured them with a thirst for learning more and more about different people, their worlds, whether real or fantastical. Books were my best friends. And today, I can see the profound impact my reading and comprehension skills have had in my life and how they continue to support me in every communication I make daily. Books not only give your child that command over language which gives him an edge in his interactions with people, but they also show him varied perspectives. They teach him about art, culture, people, relationships, emotions, attitudes, power dynamics, the workings of the world and many more life lessons that you cannot possibly learn from any one person or interaction. There is a new worldview that your child can derive from each book he reads. Your child will experience different worlds and get to live in them, and it will teach him more about himself—his likes, his dislikes, his ambitions, his limitations, his strengths, his inspirations and his motivations. Reading is the foremost component of building language development skills, and most importantly, life lessons.

✹ *Exposure to Varied Experiences*: The more places you go to, the more your child will find that there are things and people he did not know of. And with this realization, your child will find it exciting to try and understand the world he lives in. The more varied your child's experience, the more he will imbibe and comprehend, and the richer his language skills will develop. Also, by merely being around you and watching your reactions and hearing how you speak about those experiences will broaden his understanding.

✹ *Good Words and Phrases File*: When I was a child, I maintained a 'Good Words and Phrases' file where my mother or I wrote down difficult but attractive words and phrases that we liked in various books we read. Whenever I had to write an essay for school and I wanted to find a good word to express myself, I would check my file and I would use it and add to the verbal inventory in my mind. I highly encourage parents to do this with their children. It could be words that they like and want to use or even a phrase. When I like specific descriptions of people and places, I write those down too and revisit them with my son and he tries to find a way to use it in his daily interactions. It is a great reinforcement tool and adds to your child's overall knowledge base and helps aid better comprehension skills.

* *Board Games, Memory Games and Card Games*: These are great ways to introduce new concepts, categories and words to your child. The more you bond over games, the more you will expose your child to new realms of comprehension. There may be many times where he can look at an image but not know what its name, synonym, classification or use is. So, while playing, if you delve into these notions and explain them, it will enhance their understanding and increase their knowledge base.

* *Organizing Tools:* Organizing tools are excellent when it comes to giving your children a chance to rehearse their existing language components. Preparing a vision board together or a goal-setting chart or making their daily schedule or putting them in charge of listing chores on their daily responsibility chart, etc. are productive ways to converse with your child. Having many different concepts to figure out and tasks to accomplish makes them think and process various notions that promote executive brain function.

* *Word Games*: Playing games that help you express yourself or name an emotion, action or person—such as I Spy (make the other person guess an item you see around you

without taking its name), Connect (select a category and each player must name one item under that category), number or category Bingo, Spin-a-Story (pick up cards and concoct a story out of the random items you get on the cards), Name-Place-Animal-Thing (name as many items as possible under these four categories in a limited time period), Taboo (explaining a word without using the list of 'taboo' words to explain it)—help your child process and utilize their bank of words in a practical manner and rehearse the concepts they have grasped.

Music and Television: Ever heard your child scream out the words of a song verbatim without knowing their meaning? Take the time to explain the words to them and watch them use those words in their conversations with their peers or family members. We cannot deny the overwhelming amount of dependence we all have on technology in this digital age and its many boons along with its banes. However, the use of interactive educational apps can help your child process basic concepts and, similarly, certain television shows can teach your child a plethora of words and phrases. The simple act of visually processing the spoken word on a video can have a profound impact on a child's mind no less than listening to words in a conversation or reading a word in a book. It can help with character development too. These are all important for early learning and they can work wonders for your child's language development. For instance, my son often asks me what a word means and when I ask how he came upon it, he plays a song for me or tells me he heard it while watching his favourite TV show.

✳ *'Know' a Word*: They say to know a word in all its entirety, one must also know how to read and write it, in addition to just knowing how to say it. So every time your child asks the meaning of a word, show it to him by writing it down so he can read it and then ask him to think of its meaning and its opposite word. Knowing how a word is written and being able to read it out is important for comprehension and can be made fun by employing games such as Spell-a-Word or Scrabble where the words can be written or spelled out using alphabet blocks.

✳ *Pretend Play:* Pretend play is the best way to impart little titbits of information about various aspects of life that will forever be ingrained in your little one's mind. Your child will process that intelligence and attempt to use it in his daily conversations.

These are some ways that can enhance your child's vocabulary and enrich his way of thinking, his perceptions, his creative abilities and his ability to express himself. Most importantly, these will bestow upon him the crucial ability to be lucid and articulate in his conversations. In his later years, this will translate into eloquence and effective oratory power, which itself has more influence than most other skills.

EPILOGUE
WHY PLAYFUL PARENTING?

Each day of our lives, we make deposits
in the memory banks of our children.
—CHARLES SWINDOLL

As we make these 'deposits' in the banks of our children's memories, we should endeavour to make them happier, more meaningful and *playful*.

So, finally, why be the playful parent? Why engage in being the playful parent and make all of this effort with pretend play activities and scores of books and research?

Sometimes we get caught up with the entire process that parenting involves—ensuring your child is eating right, looking right, feeling right, attending classes on time, doing his homework, seeing his friends, seeing his family, visiting his doctors, brushing his teeth, avoiding too many sweets, avoiding too much screen time, getting some physical activity . . . and the list goes on and on. In this daily routine, we forget some important aspects of parenting such as being that silly goofy parent, just letting our hair down, having fun and bonding with our child! When you engage in pretend play or read to your child, with tones and inflections, and assuming characters, you are connecting with your child at his level and this creates a stronger bond between you two. It offers your relationship a new facet that creates a zone of comfort and identification.

If you got this far in this book, you now know that there are innumerable benefits to being the playful parent.

First, it helps foster a bond between parent and child. Ever seen the way your child looks at you when you act silly with him, make funny faces, get down and dirty, do a silly dance, pretend to be a monster, etc.? It is a look of identification, bemusement and wonder. When you get to their level, there is a new sense of comfort and connection that ultimately leads to increased trust, security and respect.

Second, it lightens the mood and brightens up your house. When you want to get your child to eat that meal, instead of telling him about the benefits of the food or yelling at him to eat or threatening him that you'll take away his screen time—start a card game and let him win and laugh the whole time so that he is more likely to give in and eat those unpleasant veggies and protest less.

Third, playful parenting does a great deal for increasing a child's confidence and self-esteem. When they win a game at home, they are suddenly more confident in their abilities outside the home.

Fourth, playful parenting comes with praise and positive reinforcement, which provides for holistic skill development in the early years. When you tell your child, 'That was amazing!' or 'Well done!', or use the words, 'Excellent!' or 'Fantastic!', you will see their connection with you becomes deeper. Children need to feel that deep connection in order to grow, and praise and positive reinforcements help them realize and recognize what they have done and assists with higher goal-setting and increased attempts at accomplishing the same.

Fifth, research has concluded that play scientifically engages the prefrontal cortex, which promotes executive functioning, healthy social skills, creativity and emotions. It also helps children deal with their emotions such as anger, fear, shyness and lack of confidence, and work through them at home. In fact, the Lego Foundation conducted a study that noted that discussions and interactions during playtime between children and parents help children build neural connections. So, communicating with them during play leaves a mark on their overall development and helps develop robust communication skills early on.

Sixth, children comprehend important reactions to situations by observing the behaviour of adults in the house during play. Their sense of cognitive reasoning and logical processing gets stronger as they comprehend how to respond to certain conditions by emulating their parents. It teaches them important cultural attributes, acceptance of diversity and even assigning of value to certain things that parents consider important. Many a times your child will ask you the meaning of a word or a phrase you used during play. Use that opportunity to explain it and provide a context for it. For instance, we were playing a board game and I said to my husband, 'Well, that was a real shot in the dark.' My son asked me what it meant and I explained to him that a shot in the dark is when you don't have the knowledge about something and are not really sure about the outcome of your actions but you go ahead and take a chance and guess something anyway, hoping it will stick or work. He ruminated on it for a few seconds. A few days later, when we were seated for dinner, I filled his plate with his usual dinner and I added a vegetable that I knew he did not like but tried to camouflage it with the rice. When he saw his plate, he smiled at the food he liked and then played with it for a bit. Then when he noticed the disgraceful vegetable, he said to me, 'Mom, you know I don't like this vegetable. That was a real shot in the dark.' Instantly, we erupted into laughter at the table.

Finally, being a playful parent creates a safe and loving environment, which leads to a great deal of expressiveness between the parents and the child. It is the ideal space to discuss feelings, practise reasoning, understand concepts like cause and effect, and is ultimately a superlative way of developing and shaping a young mind. Being able to put your feelings and thoughts into words is a gift that if developed early, will keep reaping rewards in adult life. For instance, while playing, a friend's child once began a very serious conversation about a terrible tooth pain she had been having for a week but had not mentioned it to anyone till it was time to play with Mommy. When they were busy playing the fool, she thought it was a safe time to discuss it with her. So, playful mommy is the most approachable mommy too.

There are compelling reasons to playfully interact with your child and teach him much more than they can learn in a typical classroom setting. Most importantly, it will help foster a healthier and a happier home, and will make you feel like a more energized, happier parent.

So, all you need to do is PLAY, BABY, PLAY!

RECOMMENDED CHILDREN'S BOOKS

You can find magic wherever you look.
Sit back and relax, all you need is a good book.
—Dr Suess.

I believe that children relate to concepts better when they read about them. Whenever I feel that, as a parent, I want to discuss a specific topic, emotion or situation, I find a book to read that can activate and spark an insightful conversation about that topic. Books can also offer fresh perspectives on things, from what an adult can offer on the topic. They cause a child to reflect, ruminate, create opinions and take decisions. I have curated a list of books (in the age group of two to seven years) that can help your child adjust, acclimatize with, transition from certain situations or merely to help him understand a particular emotion or concept.

Learning the Alphabet

- *Chicka Chicka Boom Boom* by Bill Martin Jr. and John Archambault
- *AlphaTales* Box Set

Numbers

- *Penguins Love Counting* by Sarah Aspinall
- *What's in the Piggy Bank?* by Janet Craig

Listening Skills

(On the importance of listening)

- *The Rabbit Listened* by Cori Doerrfeld

Friendship

(Books to explain the depth of good friendships and to encourage social interactions)

- *Cyril and Pat* by Emily Gravett
- *Winne the Pooh* series by A. A. Milne
- *Master Money, the Millionaire* by Allen Ahlberg and Andre Amstutz
- *Puffin Peter* by Petr Horacek
- *The Hide-and-Scare Bear* by Ivan Bates
- *Rosie Is My Best Friend* by Ali Pye
- *My Friends* by Taro Gomi
- *The Owl and the Pussycat* by Lewis Carroll and Edward Lear
- *The Lion and the Mouse* by Jerry Pinkney
- *Androcles and the Lion* by Russell Punter
- *My Friend Rabbit* by Eric Rohmann
- *The Three Pigs* by David Wiesner

☞ *The Adventures of Beekey: The Unimaginary Friend* by Dan Santat

Bath Time Phobia

☞ *101 Reasons Why I'm Not Taking a Bath* by Stacy McAnulty

Poetry

☞ *Snow* by Walter de la Mare

Fairies and Magic

☞ *The Faraway Tree* series by Enid Blyton

☞ *The Wishing Chair* series by Enid Blyton

☞ *Rainbow Magic Fairy* series by Daisy Meadows

Mystery

☞ *Famous Five* series by Enid Blyton

☞ *Noddy* series by Enid Blyton

On Modes of Transport

☞ *Little Blue Truck* by Alice Schertle

☞ *The Truck Book* by Harry McNaught

☞ *Amazing Airplanes* by Tony Mitton and Ant Parker

☞ *Off and Away* by Cale Atkinson

☞ *Mad about Trucks and Diggers* by Giles Andreae and David Wojtowycz

☞ *Busy Boats* by Campbell Books

☞ *The Mice and the Travel Machine* by Rodney Pepe

☞ *The Hundred Decker Bus* by Mike Smith

☞ *Ocean Meets Sky* by Terry Fan and Eric Fan

☞ *If I Built a Car* by Chris Van Dusen

☞ *The Great Balloon Hullaballoo* by Peter Bently and Mei Matsuoka

☞ *Brilliant Boats* by Tony Mitton and Ant Parker

Goodnight Books

☞ *Good Night Sleep Tight* by Claire Freedman and Rory Tiger

☞ *Peace at Last* by Jill Murphy

Humour

☞ *Kitchen Disco* by Claire Foges

☞ *George's Marvellous Medicine* by Roald Dahl

☞ *Don't Let the Pigeon Drive the Bus* by Mo Willems

☞ *The Adventures of the Dish and the Spoon* by Mini Grey

Easter

☞ *The Egg Tree* by Katherine Milhous

Christmas

☞ *Noah's Ark* by Peter Spier

Adventure

☞ *Hello Lighthouse* by Sophie Blackall

☞ *Wolf in the Snow* by Mathew Cordell

Family

☞ *The Baby Tree* by Sophie Blackall

☞ *How to Babysit a Grandma* and *How to Babysit a Grandpa* by Jean Reagan

☞ *Don't Be Scared Little Cub* by Jillian Harker and John Bendall-Brunello

- *On the Day You Were Born* by Debra Frasier
- *I Love You Forever* by Robert Munsch
- *The Kissing Hand* by Audrey Penn
- *You Are My I Love You* by Maryann K. Cusimano

For Fussy Eaters

- *Little Green Donkey* by Anuska Allepuz

Visual Recognition and Identification

- *Busy Town* series by Richard Scarry

First Readers and Writers

- *Pete the Cat* series by James Dean and Kimberly Dean
- *Key Words Reading Scheme* (*Peter and Jane* series) by William Murray

Grocery Shopping/Supermarket

- *At the Supermarket* by Anne Rockwell
- *Max Explains Everything: Grocery Store Expert* by Stacy McAnulty
- *Shopping with Dad* by Matt Harvey and Miriam Latimer
- *Our Corner Grocery Store* by Joanne Schwartz
- *Supermarket Zoopermarket* by Nick Sharratt
- *Supermarket* by Kathleen Krull

Construction Lovers

- *Goodnight, Goodnight Construction Site* series by Sherri Duskey Rinker and Ethan Long
- *On the Construction Site* by Carron Brown
- A Year at the Construction Site by Nicholas Harris

Laundry Love

- *Wanda's Washing Machine* by Anna McQuinn and Jan McCafferty
- *Laundry Day* by Jessixa Bagley
- *Mrs. Lather's Laundry* by Allan Ahlberg

Sharing and Caring

- *We Share Everything* by Robert Munsch
- *Pig the Pug* by Aaron Blabey
- *Maddi's Fridge* by Lois Brandt

Understanding Your Body

- *Amazing You! Getting Smart about Your Private Parts* by Gail Saltz
- *Listening to My Body* by Gabi Garcia

Love for Reading and Writing

- *Word Collector* by Peter H. Reynolds
- *Rufus the Writer* by Elizabeth Bram and Chuck Groenink
- *The Book Boat's In* by Cynthia Cotten
- *How Rocket Learned to Read* by Tad Hills
- *Library Mouse: A World to Explore* by Daniel Kirk

Loving Pets and Animals

- *The Lending Zoo* by Frank Asch
- *If Animals Kissed Good Night* by Ann Whitford Paul
- *The Paperboy* by Dav Pilkey
- *The Pawed Piper* by Michelle Robinson
- *I'll Always Love You* by Hans Wilhelm

Empathy and Kindness

- *How to Be a Friend* by Laurie Krasny Brown
- *The Day the Crayons Quit* by Drew Daywalt and Oliver Jeffers
- *Come with Me* by Holly M. McGhee
- *How to Be a Lion* by Ed Vere
- *Pass It On* by Sophy Henn
- *The Smartest Giant in Town* by Julia Donaldson
- *Adrian Simcox Does NOT Have a Horse* by Marcy Campbell
- *Grumpy Monkey* by Suzanne Lang
- *Kindness Is Cooler, Mrs. Ruler* by Margery Cuyler

Encouragement and Confidence Building

(Books that show children that it is okay to be shy, to try, to fall down and to get up again)

- *Everyone Can Learn to Ride a Bicycle* by Chris Raschka
- *Too Shy for Show-and-Tell* by Beth Bracken
- *Oh, the Places You'll Go!* by Dr. Seuss
- *The Lion Inside* by Rachel Bright and Jim Field
- *You Choose!* by Nick Sharratt and Pippa Goodhart

Apprehensions about Going to School

(These are great to read when your child is setting off to nursery or big school.)

- *Goat Goes to Playgroup* by Julia Donaldson
- *Sam Goes to School* by Mary Labatt
- *Kindergarten, Here I Come* by D. J. Steinberg
- *Curious George's First Day of School* by Margret and H.A. Rey

- *The Night Before Preschool* and *The Night Before Kindergarten* by Natasha Wing
- *A New School Year: Stories in Six Voices* by Sally Derby
- *Make Way for Dyamonde Daniel* by Nikki Grimes
- *Show and Tell* by Robert Munsch
- *The Day You Begin* by Jacqueline Woodson
- *David Goes to School* by David Shannon
- *I Am Too Absolutely Small for School* by Lauren Child
- *Llama Llama Misses Mama* by Anne Dewdney
- *Bob and Flo* by Rebecca Ashdown
- *Timothy Goes to School* by Rosemary Wells

How Babies Are Made
(age appropriate; without too many details)

- *What's the Big Secret?* by Laurie Krasny Brown

On Disagreements with Your Parents
(showing children that it is normal to have arguments or difference of opinions with your family)

- *Where the Wild Things Are* by Maurice Sendak
- *Llama Llama, Mad at Mama* by Anna Dewdney

On Diversity and Cultural Differences

- *One Family* by George Shannon
- *All Are Welcome* by Alexandra Penfold and Suzanne Kaufman
- *Chocolate Milk, Por Favor!* by Maria Dismondy and Nancy Raines Day
- *The Undefeated* by Kwame Alexander and Kadir Nelson

- *Name Jar* by Yangsook Choi
- *Incredible Me!* by Kathi Appelt
- *It's Okay to Be Different* by Todd Parr
- *Mixed Blessing: A Children's Book about a Multi-Racial Family* by Marsha Cosman
- *Smoky Night* by Eve Bunting
- *Grandfather's Journey* by Allen Say
- *And Tango Makes Three* by Justin Richardson
- *Julián is a Mermaid* by Jessica Love

On the Death of a Loved One

- *The Invisible String* by Patricia Karst
- *The Rough Patch* by Brian Lies
- *The Goodbye Book* by Todd Parr
- *When I feel Sad* by Cornelia Maude Spelman
- *Scaredy Squirrel* by Melanie Watt
- *The Heart and the Bottle* by Oliver Jeffers

Career Goals

- *The Wonderful Things You Will Be* by Emily Winfield Martin
- *The Career* series by Andrea Beaty (*Iggy Peck Architect, Rosie Reverie Engineer, Ada Twist Scientist,* etc.)
- *If I Built a . . .* (House/Car/School) series by Chris Van Dusen
- *The Dot* by Peter Reynolds
- *The Invention of Hugo Cabret* by Brian Selznick

Acceptance of a New Sibling

- *You Were the First* by Patricia MacLachlan
- *I Am a Big Sister* by Caroline Jayne Church
- *Big Brother Daniel* by Angela C. Santomero

- *Just Me and My Little Brother* by Mercer Mayer
- *The New Baby* by Mercer Mayer
- *My New Baby* by Rachel Fuller

Dealing with Moods and Feelings

- *When I'm Feeling* series by Trace Moroney
- *Lou Knows What to Do* series by Kimberly Tice and Venita Litvack
- *Mummy's Suitcase* by Pip Jones
- *Enemy Pie* by Derek Munson
- *The Unbudgeable Curmudgeon* by Matthew Burgess
- *Millie Fierce* by Jane Manning
- *The Way I Feel* by Janan Cain
- *When Sophie Gets Angry—Really, Really Angry* by Molly Bang
- *What to Do When You Are Feeling Blue* by Andi Cann
- *The Bear Under the Stairs* by Helen Cooper
- *But Not the Hippopotamus* by Sandra Boynton

Dealing with Bullying, Comparisons with Other Children, Divorce, etc.

- *My Friend Maggie* by Hannah E. Harrison
- *Those Shoes* by Maribeth Boelts
- *The Juice Box Bully* by Bob Sornson and Maria Dismondy
- *Simon's Hook* by Karen Gedig Burnett
- *Was It the Chocolate Pudding?* by Sandra Levins
- *Willie the Wimp* by Anthony Browne

Attachment to a Nanny

- *Nanny and Me* by Florence Ann Romano

Inspirational Books

- *We Are Water Protectors* by Carole Lindstrom
- *So You Want to Be President?* by Judith St. George
- *Once a Mouse* by Marcia Brown
- *Prayer for a Child* by Rachel Field
- *Six Dots: A Story of Young Louis Braille* by Jen Bryant
- *Earmuffs for Everyone! How Chester Greenwood Became Known as the Inventor of Earmuffs* by Meghan McCarthy
- *Marvellous Mattie: How Margaret E. Knight became an Inventor* by Emily Arnold McCully
- *A Boy and a Jaguar* by Alan Rabinowitz
- *Ada's Violin: The Story of the Recycled Orchestra of Paraguay* by Susan Hood
- *Malala: Activist for Girls' Education* by Raphaelle Frier
- *Salt in His Shoes: Michael Jordan in Pursuit of a Dream* by Deloris Jordan
- *Little People, Big Dreams* series by Isabel Sanchez Vegara
- *How to Catch a Star* by Oliver Jeffers
- *Ordinary People Change the World* series by Brad Metzler and Christopher Eliopoulos (*I am Anne Frank, I am Frida Kalho, I am Kind,* etc.)
- *Little Heroes of Colour* by David Heredia
- *Fantastically Great Women Who Have Changed the World* by Kate Pankhurst
- *What Do You Do With . . .* (an Idea/Problem/Chance?) series by Kobi Yamada
- *Jabari Jumps* by Gaia Cornwall
- *Only One You* by Linda Kranz

On Overcoming Obstacles

- *The Book of Mistakes* by Corinna Luyken
- *When Sophie Thinks She Can't* by Molly Bang
- *Whistle for Willie* by Ezra Jack Keats
- *Thanks for the Feedback, I Think* by Julia Cook

On Dealing with Challenging Current Events

- *Corona (the Germ)* by Sophie Morris
- *Why?* by Nikolai Popov
- *Mama's Nightingale: A Story of Immigration and Separation* by Edwidge Danticat
- *Our House is on Fire: Greta Thunberg's Call to Save the Planet* by Jeanette Winter

Good Behaviour

- *Hands Are Not for Hitting* by Martine Agassi

On dealing with gender or sexual identity

- *Elena's Serenade* by Campbell Geeslin

Recycling

- *Joseph Had a Little Overcoat* by Simms Taback

ACKNOWLEDGEMENTS

It takes a village to raise a child, they say. And they are not wrong. But it also took a village to support me while I endeavoured to write this book.

This book would not have been possible without the conviction that my literary agent, Kanishka Gupta, and my editor, Meru Gokhale, had in my idea for this book without even having read a sentence. Their faith in me has given me a great deal of confidence in what started out as a simple hypothesis. I would like to thank the entire team at Penguin Random House India for believing in this book and for making it happen in the midst of a pandemic.

Special thanks to my biggest supporter, cheerleader, my raison dêtre, my soulmate, my husband Karan (who also had a part in making me a parent), for giving me my greatest reason to smile. His magnanimous love, supportive nature and encouragement are the reasons I can do what I do. I am forever grateful for that moment when we met at the age of nineteen; it has been a magical ride ever since. I am especially indebted to him for convincing me to get back to writing after I lost my desire to write along with my father.

Deeply grateful to my love, my strength, my charming little five-year-old, Kiaan, who is my ray of 'son'shine in this world. His innocence, curiosity, creativity and kindness fuel me and make every moment of my life wonderful. This journey of parenting has been so beautiful and felt so effortless—thanks to his cooperative nature.

I am grateful to my primary literary inspiration and the person who cultivated in me a love for books, words and phrases, and who inculcated a curiosity for the intricacies of the English language in me since I was a child—my mother Kareena. Without her introducing me to writers such as Enid Blyton, Shakespeare, Jane Austen, Daphne Du Maurier and Ayn Rand very early on, my life would have been flavourless.

I would like to thank my father for being a beacon of strength, resolve and inspiration to me and for nurturing that special connection and an unforgettable parent-child bond between us—it means everything to me. Every fiber of my being misses him and I am grateful for having been loved and taught by him.

My sister, Tanya, who grudgingly allowed me to parent her, thus allowing me my first experience of selfless love for a reluctant child, which adequately prepared me for parenthood.

My parents-in-law, Bijal and Sunil, who have treated me like a daughter and have always powered and encouraged me in every phase of life.

To all my wonderful friends-like-family who have stood by me through thick and thin, and who have supported my every endeavour—this book has only been possible because of your endless encouragement and, most importantly, your babysitting skills.

To every teacher and professor I ever had in school, journalism school and law school, who helped develop my literary prowess and gave me more books to dwell in—I am forever indebted to you for helping me become a parent who reads and writes.

Finally, to every mother out there who suffers from mom guilt, mom shame and self-doubt every single day—this book is a dedication to you and your unrelenting efforts at dealing with motherhood every single day. I sincerely hope you use this book to spend constructive time with your child, remembering that it is the conversation that you have with them and what you do together that defines them, and not the number of hours you spend with them. The activities in this book are not meant to make you feel less than any other mother who does more than you in a day. The process of pretend play with your child is meant to be savoured. It is meant to be enjoyed. It is meant to bring about a great deal of conversation and laughter. It is meant to show each one of us that parenting is not a competition. It is a beautiful journey that is meant to be relished at every stage. The minute you accept that every child will come to his own in his own time, that is the day you start enjoying the parenting process.

As Sue Atkins has famously said, 'There's no such thing as a perfect parent, so just be a real one.'

REFERENCES

1. Ashiabi, G.S. (2007). Play in the preschool classroom: Its socioemotional significance and the teacher's role in play. *Early Childhood Education Journal.*

2. Bodrova, E. (2008). Make-Believe play versus academic skills: A Vygotskian approach to today's dilemma of early childhood education. *European Early Childhood Education Research Journal.*

3. Berk, L. E., Mann, T.D., & Ogan, A.T. (2006). Make-Believe play: Wellspring for development of self-regulation. In D. Singer, R.M. Golinkoff, & Hirsh-Pasek (Eds.), *Play = Learning: How play motivates and enhances children's cognitive and social-emotional growth.* New York, NY: Oxford University Press.

4. Clements, D.H., & Sarama., J. (2009). *Learning and teaching early math: The learning trajectories approach.* New York, NY: Routledge.

5. Ginsburg, H. P. (2006). Mathematical play and playful mathematics: A guide for early education. In D. Singer,

R. M. Golinkoff, & K. Hirsh-Pasek (Eds.), *Play = Learning: How play motivates and enhances children's cognitive and social-emotional growth*, New York, NY: Oxford University Press, USA.

6. Hirsh-Pasek, K., Golinkoff, R.M., Berk, L.E., & Singer, D.G. (2009). *A mandate for playful learning in preschool: Presenting the evidence.* New York: Oxford University Press.

7. Hughes, F.P. (1999). *Children, play, and development* (3rd ed.). Needham Heights, MA: Allyn & Bacon.

8. Jenkins, J.M., & Astington, J.W. (2000). Theory of mind and social behavior: Casual models tested in a longitudinal study. *Merrill-Palmer Quarterly.*

9. Jent, J.F., Niec, L.N., & Baker, S.E. (2011). Play and interpersonal processes. In S.W. Russ & L.N. Niec (Eds.), *Play in clinical practice: Evidence-based approaches.* New York, NY: Guilford Press.

10. Leslie, A.M. (1987). Pretense and representation: The origins of "theory of mind". *Psychological Review.*

11. Root-Bernstein, M. (2012). The creation of imaginary worlds. In M. Taylor (Ed.), *The Oxford handbook of the development of imagination.* Oxford: Oxford University Press.

12. Russ, S.W. (2004). *Play in child development and psychotherapy.* Mahwah, NJ: Earlbaum.

13. Russ, S., & Fiorelli, J. (2010). Developmental approaches to creativity. In J. Kaufman & R. Sternberg (Eds.) *The Cambridge Handbook of Creativity,* New York: Cambridge University Press.

14. Shmukler, D. (1981). Mother-child interaction and its relationship to the predisposition of imaginative play. *Genetic Psychology Monographs.*

15. Seja, A.L., & Russ, S.W. (1999). Children's fantasy play and emotional understanding. *Journal of Clinical Child Psychology.*

16. Singer, D. G., & Singer, J. L. (1990). *The house of make believe: Children's play and the developing imagination.* Cambridge, MA: Harvard University Press.

17. Singer, D.G. & Singer, J.L. (2005). *Imagination and play in the electronic age.* Cambridge, MA: Harvard University Press.

18. Singer, D. G., Singer, J. L., Plaskon, S. L., & Schweder, A. E. (2003). The role of play in the preschool curriculum. In S. Olfman (Ed.), *All work and no play: How educational reforms are harming our preschoolers.* Westport, CT: Praeger Publishers.

19. Singer, J.L., & Lythcott, M.A. (2004). Fostering school achievement and creativity through sociodramatic play in the classroom. In E. F. Zigler, D.G. Singer, & S. J. Bishop-Joseph (Eds.), *Children's play: The roots of reading* (pp. 77-93). Washington DC: Zero to Three Press.

20. Slade, S., & Wolf, D. P. (1999). *Play: Clinical and developmental approaches to meaning and representation.* Oxford University Press.

21. Weitzman, E., & Greenberg, J. (2010). *ABC and beyond: Building emergent literacy in early childhood settings.* Toronto: The Hanen Centre.

22. Rowe, M. (2012). A longitudinal investigation of the role of quantity and quality of child-directed speech in vocabulary development. *Child Development Journal.*

23. Hart, B., & Risley, T.R. (1995). *Meaningful differences in the everyday experiences of young American children.* Baltimore: Paul H. Brookes Publishing Co.

24. The Lego Foundation. (2019). *What we mean by: Playful parenting in the early years.* Lego Foundation.